Critical Guides to French Texts

88 Flaubert: Trois **Contes**

Critical Guides to French Texts

EDITED BY ROGER LITTLE, WOLFGANG VAN EMDEN,
DAVID WILLIAMS

FLAUBERT

Trois Contes

A.W. Raitt

Fellow of Magdalen College
and Reader in French Literature
in the University of Oxford

Grant & Cutler Ltd
1991

© Grant & Cutler Ltd 1991

ISBN 0 7293 0334 9

I.S.B.N. 84-599-3247-8

DEPÓSITO LEGAL: V. 2.742 - 1991

Printed in Spain by
Artes Gráficas Soler, S.A., Valencia
for
GRANT & CUTLER LTD
55-57 GREAT MARLBOROUGH STREET, LONDON W1V 2AY

Contents

Note on Texts

There are many good and easily accessible editions of *Trois Contes*. The one I have chosen to quote from is the excellent 1986 Garnier-Flammarion edition by P.-M. de Biasi, but I have also quoted from other editions where they offer material not included by Biasi (see Bibliography). Page references to the Biasi edition are given in brackets in the texts. The references to other works listed in the bibliography give the number of the book or article in italics, with the volume number (where necessary) in roman numerals followed by the page number.

Introduction

When he was an adolescent, Gustave Flaubert wrote a number of short stories – historical, satirical, horrific and psychological – but as he matured, his ambitions turned more and more towards the novel and for many years he paid scant attention to the shorter genre. Even in his novels the story-telling element is not especially to the fore – he once declared to the Goncourt brothers: 'l'histoire, l'aventure d'un roman, ça m'est bien égal. J'ai la pensée, quand je fais un roman, de rendre une coloration, une nuance' (*60*, I, pp.888-89). Likewise, his correspondence is sparing of anecdotes. Though from time to time he seems to have thought of composing a short story, he did not have the irresistible penchant for telling stories which governed the vocation of writers such as Mérimee, Maupassant and Villiers de l'Isle-Adam. It was thus largely chance which brought him to write the *Trois Contes*, which were published in 1877 and form his last completed work (he died suddenly in 1880 at the age of 58, in the middle of the immense labour entailed by his encyclopaedic novel *Bouvard et Pécuchet*).

In effect it was depression and loss of confidence which led him at this late stage to turn to a less ambitious genre than the novel. The preceding years had been particularly dark. In 1869, *L'Education sentimentale* had met with incomprehension and indignation. In 1874, his play *Le Candidat* had failed so ignominiously that he had withdrawn it after four performances, and a few weeks later *La Tentation de Saint Antoine*, always his favourite work and now in its third version, was greeted with derision. Though Flaubert was not much concerned with plaudits and public admiration, he was deeply hurt by this series of setbacks. He had at the same time felt shattered by the defeat of his country in the Franco-Prussian War and by the trauma of the Commune. Added to all this, he had lost several of his closest friends: his devoted collaborator Louis Bouilhet in 1869, Jules de Goncourt in 1870, Théophile Gautier in 1872. Worst of all, his mother, to whom he was deeply attached and with whom he lived, had died in 1872. Then in 1874 Ernest Commanville, the husband of his beloved niece Caroline, whom he had largely brought up after his sister's death, got into difficulties with his timber business, so that Flaubert, who had always enjoyed financial independence and had never had to live by his pen, felt obliged to sacrifice his fortune so as to save the Commanvilles from bankruptcy and disgrace. This happened when he was still in the early stages of *Bouvard et Pécuchet* which, after years of doubt and hesitation, he had finally started to write in 1872. But he was already worn down by the difficulties of the task, and work had been progressing with excruciating slowness, the more so as he was unconvinced of the viability of the enterprise. So, when the hitherto solid structure of his world collapsed about his ears, he sank into a profound depression, unable to think of anything save the bleakness of his future and so incapable of facing up again to the over-daunting challenge of *Bouvard et Pécuchet* that he at first thought he would never be able to resume writing at all.

It was in these circumstances that he decided to take his mind off his worries by going for a holiday by the sea, at Concarneau in Brittany, with Georges Pouchet, a naturalist friend. He arrived on 16 September 1875 and at first did nothing but watch the fishing boats in the harbour, bathe and accompany Pouchet to his laboratory – having left all his pens and paper at home. But before long he was overcome by the need to write again, and while the thought of *Bouvard et Pécuchet* was still too much for him, he believed he might manage something less demanding, especially if it was totally remote from his present preoccupations. Hence his turning to the story of St Julian the Hospitaller (or Hospitator), a hagiographical legend familiar to him for many years and which he had planned and prepared in some detail in 1856. The subject was thus in a sense predigested and the planning stage was therefore relatively painless. But he was working without enthusiasm and largely for therapeutic purposes: 'je ferai cela comme un pensum, pour voir ce qui en résultera' (25 September 1975; *1*, XV, p.408), 'le foi n'y est plus, on ne résiste pas à des coups pareils' (2 October 1875; *1*, XV, p.412), 'c'est pour m'occuper et pour voir si je peux encore faire une phrase, – ce dont je doute' (8 October 1875; *1*, XV, p.413). The actual writing was as slow and difficult as it had been for all his novels from Madame Bovary onwards, so despite his disparaging remarks about the tale – 'ma petite historiette' (14 October 1875; *1*, XV, p.420), 'Ce n'est rien du tout, et je n'y attache aucune importance' (2 October 1875; *1*, XV, p.410), 'une petite bêtise *moyenâgeuse*' (16 December 1875; *1*, XV, p.429), 'une petite niaiserie' (December 1875; *1*, XV, p.431) – he was treating it just as seriously as his major works.

By early February he was nearing the end of *La Légende de Saint Julien l'Hospitalier* and had convinced himself he could write again, but still felt too shaken to return to *Bouvard et Pécuchet* or undertake another full-length novel: 'je suis trop profondément ébranlé pour me mettre à une grande oeuvre' (6 February 1876; *1*, XV, p.435). It was at this stage that he thought of resurrecting another short tale, the subject of which had occurred to him some years previously. This was what was to become *Un Cœur simple*, and his idea was that the two tales together would form a slim volume which could be published that autumn. By mid-February, *Saint Julien* was finished and work on the next tale had begun. Progress was delayed by floods which prevented him from travelling to Normandy to refresh his memories of the places in which the story was to be set. However, before he had got much further, he decided to add a third short work, and by mid-April he knew this next subject would be the execution of St John the Baptist. This too was not a new subject; evidently he had had the idea in 1871. He completed *Un Cœur simple* in the middle of August 1876 and at once embarked on an extensive programme of documentation for *Hérodias*, which occupied him for well over a month, so that composition only started in October and lasted until the end of January 1877.

Despite his reluctance to publish in newspapers, Flaubert resigned himself for financial reasons to allowing the tales to appear in the press, so that *Un Cœur simple* came out in *Le Moniteur universel* from 12 to 19 April, followed by *Hérodias* from 21 to 27 April, while *Saint Julien* was published in *Le Bien public* from 19 to 22 April. Thanks to Turgeniev, Russian translations appeared simultaneously. The book was brought out by Charpentier immediately afterwards.

The history of the genesis of *Trois Contes* makes clear a number of significant points. The first is that these tales are the product of the maturity of a great writer, who already had the bulk of his major works behind him, but at the same time that all three subjects had ripened in his mind over a period of years. The second is that, though the stories were written because he did not feel strong enough to devote himself to a long novel, he treated them with the same conscientiousness as his novels. Thirdly, the three stories were conceived separately and the volume as a whole only took shape gradually and was not planned as a unit from the outset. Finally, the order in which the stories are printed is not that of their composition; it is therefore appropriate to consider them in the order in which Flaubert wished them to be read.

2. Un Cœur simple

Though *Un Cœur simple* was not written until 1876 and may seem to be an exception in Flaubert's work, in its obviously sympathetic portrayal of Félicité, it has a number of forerunners in his writings. The first of these occurs in *Rage et impuissance*, a tale written in 1836, in which there is an incidental character of an old maidservant, described in these terms: 'C'est dans ses souvenirs d'enfance qu'errait ainsi son imagination, et la vieille Berthe se retraçait ainsi toute sa vie, qui s'était passée monotone et uniforme dans son village et qui, dans un cercle si étroit, avait eu aussi ses passions, ses angoisses et ses douleurs' (*1*, XI, p.264). The idea of writing about the hidden drama in apparently monotonous lives reappears in *Par les champs et par les grèves*, his 1847 account of his travels in Brittany, where a quiet street in Blois inspires these reflections: 'On se plaît à rêver, dans ces paisibles demeures, quelque profonde et grande histoire intime, une passion maladive qui dure jusqu'à la mort, amour contenu de vieille fille ou de femme vertueuse' (*1*, X, p.32). By 1849 or 1850, the subject was taking more definite shape, and to Louis Bouilhet, Flaubert talked about 'mon roman flamand de la jeune fille qui meurt vierge et mystique entre son père et sa mère, dans une petite ville de province, au fond d'un jardin planté de choux et de quenouilles, au bord d'une rivière grande comme l'eau de Robec', adding that the story would turn on earthly and mystical love: 'ils sont réunis dans la même personne, et l'un mène à l'autre, seulement mon héroïne crève de masturbation religieuse après avoir exercé la masturbation digitale' (14 November 1850; *1*, XIII, p.95). Years later, in less crude terms he confided to a woman friend that it was out of this idea that *Madame Bovary* had developed: 'L'idée première que j'avais eue était d'en faire une vierge vivant au milieu de la province, vieillissant dans le chagrin et arrivant ainsi aux derniers états du mysticisme et de la passion rêvée. J'ai gardé de ce premier plan tout l'entourage (paysages et personnages assez noirs), la couleur enfin. Seulement, pour rendre l'histoire plus compréhensible et plus amusante au bon sens du mot, j'ai inventé une histoire plus humaine, une femme comme on en voit davantage. J'entrevoyais d'ailleurs dans l'exécution de ce premier plan de telles difficultés que je n'ai pas osé' (30 March 1857; *1*, XIII, p.570). In 1861, he confirmed to the Goncourt brothers that shortly before starting work on Madame Bovary, he had conceived it quite differently: 'Ce devait être, dans le même milieu et la même tonalité, une vieille fille dévote et ne baisant pas. Et puis j'ai compris que ce serait un personnage impossible' (*60*, I, p.889).

But if Flaubert changed his mind about the central character, no doubt in part because the original idea would hardly have yielded enough incident for a novel, it is possible that something of it survives in *Madame Bovary* in the person of Catherine Leroux, the humble, pious old woman who, at the Comices Agricoles, is given a medal for fifty years' service on the same farm. She is described with patent sympathy in terms much akin to those used about Félicité, but the last sentence of the passage vibrates with barely contained fury against the hated bourgeois responsible for so much suffering and hardship: 'Ainsi se tenait devant ces bourgeois épanouis ce demi-siècle de servitude' (*1*, I, p.184). It is instructive to compare this indignant conclusion with the first sentence of *Un Cœur simple*, where the same elements are assembled in a tone of carefully controlled neutrality: 'Pendant un demi-siècle, les bourgeoises de Pont-l'Evêque envièrent à Mme Aubain sa servante Félicité' (p.43).

But at some stage an analogous subject entered his mind, that of the devotion of an old maidservant for a parrot (perhaps suggested by the relationship between a commercial traveller and a sick parakeet he had noted in 1845 with the comment: 'Quel singulier amour!', *1*, X, p.362). This idea was sketched out in a plan headed *Perroquet*, which briefly relates Félicité's attachment to the parrot, even after its death, and her own death during the Corpus Christi procession, ending with a dialogue between Félicité and the priest: ' "Il m'a semblé que les chaînettes des encensoirs étaient le bruit de sa chaîne. Est-ce un péché mon père... Non, mon enfant". / Et elle expira' (*1*, IV, pp.431-32). It is not known when this plan was drawn up: various dates between 1853 and 1864 have been suggested but the evidence is inconclusive.[1]

What seems to have happened is that, casting around for the subject of another short tale which was all he felt capable of undertaking after Saint Julien, he bethought himself of the story of the maid's fetishistic devotion to the parrot, and at the same time realised that this could be amalgamated with something of the theme of the 'roman flamand' which he had considered writing in 1850. The absence of action and incident which rendered the subject unsuitable for a novel would not be a drawback in a much shorter work.

There are, however, special reasons why, at that point in his life, he should have chosen to treat an idea which would give expression to feelings of tenderness about a sympathetic character. These lie in the running argument he had been conducting for years with George Sand about the aims of literature, with Flaubert upholding his ideal of impersonality while Sand defended a conception of art which would be more emotive and less depressing for the reader. She seems at last to have got under his skin when, in December 1875, talking of their respective projects, she said: 'Toi à coup sûr, tu vas faire de la *désolation* et moi de la *consolation*' (*63*, p.511). Flaubert's rejoinder was indignant: 'Je ne fais pas 'de la désolation' à plaisir! croyez-le bien! mais je ne peux pas changer mes yeux!' (*1*, XV, p.430). But in her next letter, she returned to the attack with pressing advice: 'Ne prends pas la vertu vraie pour un lieu commun en littérature. Donne-lui son représentant, fais passer l'honnête et le fort à travers ces fous et ces idiots dont tu aimes à te moquer. Montre ce qui est solide au fond de ces avortements intellectuels' (*63*, p.519). It is surely no coincidence that, in his reply to this letter Flaubert announces his intention of writing what was to become *Un Cœur simple*. When one takes this sequence of events in conjunction with his later declarations – to George Sand that 'Vous verrez par mon *Histoire d'un cœur simple* où

---

[1]This plan was originally discovered by Alberto Cento (*19*, p.103), who tentatively suggested 1853 or 1864 as possible dates. More recently, Giovanni Bonaccorso (*28*, p.lii) has proposed 1856, a hypothesis also adopted by P.M. Wetherill (*5*, p.308). Other commentators who have mentioned this plan (Bardèche, *1*, IV, p.429, Willenbrink, *24*, p.68 and Fleury, *25*, p.94) do not attempt to date it. Because the evidence is so slender, it is no doubt prudent to refrain from any conclusions.

vous reconnaîtrez votre influence immédiate que je ne suis pas si entêté que vous le croyez. Je crois que la tendance morale, ou plutôt le dessous humain de cette petite œuvre vous sera agréable',[2] and after her death, to her son Maurice: 'J'avais commencé *Un Cœur simple* à son intention exclusive, uniquement pour lui plaire' (*1*, XV, p.593) – it seems clear what induced him to tackle the subject in the way he did.

On the one hand, he refused to forsake his pessimism or his views on the harshness of the world: that would have been dishonest. On the other hand, he wanted to demonstrate to George Sand that, even within that context, it was possible to focus on an exception, to portray an admirable character whose life could in some sense be accounted a success. It was evidently in these circumstances that he remembered the pity he had already shown for characters like Catherine Leroux and resolved to construct a story which would show a virtuous and sympathetic character being rewarded with happiness, rather than crushed and destroyed by life. That is why he turned to a person of no culture, no imagination, no real intelligence, for his central figure: too much lucidity would have enabled her to see her position from the outside and would have ruined that 'tranquillité de son âme, récompense de sa vertu' (*1*, IV, p.433), which a marginal note on a draft explicitly picks out as one of the keys to her life. Hence the paradox of her name and situation: 'Félicité' may be taken in its literal sense if one considers the inner calm which characterises her and the celestial reward which is her lot in the end, or it may be considered ironic if, from the outside, one considers her poverty, her successive frustrations, her loneliness. In this perspective, the final vision of the parrot welcoming her into heaven is deliberately ambivalent: 'elle crut voir, dans les cieux entrouverts, un perroquet gigantesque, planant au-dessus de sa tête' (p.78). This non-committal formula, with the crucial 'crut', leaves it open whether what she sees is a hallucination or a genuine vision. By this device, Flaubert holds back from a definite authorial view. If we wish, we can dismiss the apotheosis as a delusion of a sick mind – but, from Félicité's point of view, that does not matter.

[2]This letter is not in the Club de l'Honnête Homme edition. See A. Jacobs (*63*, p.533). It is not clear why Jacobs (p.11) should be reluctant to accept that *Un Cœur simple* was decisively influenced by George Sand: the evidence is concordant, and there is no reason to mistrust it.

If her vision is an illusion, at least it is a consoling illusion, and it remains intact, whereas the dominating theme of Madame Bovary had precisely been the destruction of illusions, and there is an exemplary contrast between the beatific vision which Félicité has as she dies, and the horrific image which fills the eyes of the dying Emma: 'Et Emma se mit à rire, d'un rire atroce, frénétique, désespéré, croyant voir la face hideuse du misérable qui se dressait dans les ténèbres éternelles comme un épouvantement' (*1*, I, p.337).

There is thus a double rhythm in *Un Cœur simple*, on the level of events as on the level of style. One rhythm is that of frustration and disappointment: the betrayal by Théodore, the death of Virginie, the departure of Paul, the disappearance of Victor, the death of the parrot, the loss of her faculties, and this is echoed stylistically by the recurrence of the falling cadence, the sentence or paragraph which leads one to expect fulfilment and climax, and which suddenly stops short and breaks off unexpectedly, as in these examples recounting the departure of Victor's ship and the death of Virginie: 'Sa membrure craquait, les vagues pesantes fouettaient sa proue. La voile avait tourné, on ne vit plus personne; – et, sur la mer argentée par la lune, il faisait une tache noire qui pâlissait toujours, s'enfonça, disparut' (p.58); 'Trois chandeliers sur la commode faisaient des taches rouges, et le brouillard blanchissait les fenêtres. Des religieuses emportèrent Mme Aubain' (p.63). Yet the story as a whole moves to a magnificent peak at the end: the longest sentence of all evokes the Corpus Christi procession. Flaubert announced in advance his intention to 'finir ma *Félicité* d'une façon splendide' (*1*, XV, p.481), and to have at the end 'une phrase très longue' before he had even decided what it was going to say. Once again the contrast with what happens elsewhere is revealing: one thinks of the offbeat irony of the end of *Madame Bovary*: 'Il vient de recevoir la croix d'honneur' (*1*, I, p.357), or the casually hesitant conclusion of *L'Education sentimentale*: ' "Oui, peut-être bien? c'est là ce que nous avons eu de meilleur!" dit Deslauriers' (*1*, III, p.399).

What enables Félicité to preserve her inner equilibrium through so many sorrows and misfortunes, and justifies the eventual transcendental reward which Flaubert bestows on her, is what in the drafts he identifies, in those abstract generalising terms he avoids in the finished text, as 'son besoin d'aimer' (*1*, IV, p.447). This comes out in the way in which he summarises the tale for Mme Roger Des Genettes: '*L'Histoire d'un cœur simple* est tout bonnement le récit d'une vie obscure, celle d'une pauvre fille de campagne, dévote mais pas mystique, dévouée sans exaltation et tendre comme du pain frais. Elle aime successivement un homme, les enfants de sa maîtresse, un neveu, un vieillard qu'elle soigne, puis son perroquet; quand le perroquet est mort, elle le fait empailler et, en mourant à son tour, elle confond le perroquet avec le Saint-Esprit. Cela n'est nullement ironique comme vous le supposez, mais au contraire très sérieux et très triste. Je veux apitoyer, faire pleurer les âmes sensibles, en étant une moi-même' (19 June 1876; *1*, XV, p.457-58). That this remark is not purely jocular is confirmed by his pleasure when, after a reading of the story, Auguste Sabatier, by being '*ému*', showed he had 'si bien compris mes intentions' (3 August 1876; *1*, XV, p.480), and by his comment to Mme Husson that, on the publication of the story, 'Loin de passer pour un porc (ce qui est en partie le point de vue sous lequel les bourgeois m'envisagent), on dira, au contraire, que je suis un 'homme sensible'. Ce qui est vrai, hélas!' (28 July 1876; *1*, XV, p.477). He was even quite indignant when his old friend Mrs Tennant seemed sceptical about the genuineness of the emotion in the story: 'Pourquoi paraissez-vous étonnée de ce que j'aie pu faire un conte intitulé: *Un Cœur simple*? Votre ébahissement m'intrigue. Douteriez-vous de mes facultés de tendresse? Vous n'avez pas ce droit-là, vous!' (16 February 1877; *1*, XV, p.540).

In fact, the succession of loves is carefully gradated. First, love for a man whom she believes to love her, then love for her employer's children, then love for the son of a sister whom she scarcely knows: then love for other human beings with whom she has no normal family or affective connections, a revolting old pauper dying in a hovel, marching soldiers, cholera victims, Polish refugees; then for a living animal in the shape of Loulou the parrot; and finally for an inanimate object, the stuffed parrot which becomes ever more dilapidated. What strikes one in all these cases is that there is never any reciprocity: Théodore courts her for his sexual gratification, Mme Aubain and her children treat her with coolness and indifference, Victor and his mother are seeking to get out of her what they can, the old pauper dies, the cholera victims and the refugees pass out of her life; the parrot, by its talk, provides her with only the illusion of companionship: 'Ils avaient des dialogues, lui débitant à satiété les trois phrases de son répertoire, et elle, y répondant par des mots sans plus de suite, mais où son cœur s'épanchait' (p.70). And, once the parrot is dead and stuffed, it is merely an object among other objects, as is made clear by the long catalogue in which Flaubert lists the contents of Félicité's bedroom, where the parrot has pride of place among things as diverse as old furniture, the trappings of popular piety, the relics of the children Félicité has loved, and meaningless pieces of junk such as an out-of-date royalist picture.

So at all times Félicité's affections are totally selfless, she neither expects nor receives anything in return, but constantly lives in others, outside herself. Though Flaubert scrupulously refrains from pointing morals, there can be little doubt that, in his view, this is the best way to live. Again he is more explicit in the drafts, where one reads: 'Son genre de bonheur. / Son calme. / Pour que ce soit la moralité de l'histoire, qu'on ait envie de l'imiter' (*1*, IV, p.447). It is indeed very much the advice he proffered to his niece while working on *Un Cœur simple*: 'Autant que possible, il ne faut jamais rêver qu'à un objet en dehors de nous; autrement on tombe dans l'océan des tristesses' (*1*, XV, p.471). Echoes of this attitude are perceptible in his novels too, as when in *L'Education sentimentale* the unhappy Frédéric Moreau finds momentary peace by immersing himself (albeit incompetently) in the absurdly ambitious project of composing an *Histoire de la Renaissance*: 'Peu à peu, la sérénité du travail l'apaisa. En plongeant dans la personnalité des autres, il oublia la sienne, ce qui est la seule manière peut-être de n'en pas souffrir' (*1*, III, p.199). In the original text of *Madame Bovary*, Flaubert had likewise taken Rodolphe severely to task for his failure to comprehend the selflessness of true love: 'Car il ne comprenait rien (...) à la passion vide d'orgueil, sans respect humain, ni conscience, qui plonge tout entière dans l'être aimé, accapare ses sentiments, en palpite et touche aux proportions d'une idée pure, à force de largeur et d'impersonnalité' (*59*, p.641).

Expressions such as this forcibly remind us that Flaubert hated being Flaubert and that, far from using impersonality as a literary technique, he used literature as a means of being impersonal, of ceasing to be Gustave Flaubert and of being, instead, Emma, Félicité, St Julien, Antipas. There is a famous letter in which he describes writing the seduction scene between Rodolphe and Emma: 'c'est une délicieuse chose que d'écrire! que de ne plus être soi, mais de circuler dans toute la création dont on parle. Aujourd'hui, par exemple, homme et femme tout ensemble, amant et maîtresse à la fois, je me suis promené à cheval dans une forêt, par un après-midi d'automne, sous les feuilles jaunes, et j'étais les chevaux, les feuilles, le vent, les paroles qu'ils se disaient et le soleil rouge qui faisait s'entre-fermer leurs paupières noyées d'amour' (*1*, XII, p.442). There is an obvious analogy here with Félicité's reactions when watching Virginie make her First Communion: 'Quand ce fut le tour de Virginie, Félicité se pencha pour la voir, et, avec l'imagination que donnent les vraies tendresses, il lui sembla qu'elle était elle-même cette enfant, sa figure devenait la sienne, sa robe l'habillait, son cœur lui battait dans sa poitrine (...) Le lendemain, de bonne heure, elle se présenta dans la sacristie, pour que M. le Curé lui donnât la communion. Elle la reçut dévotement, mais n'y goûta pas les mêmes délices' (pp.55-56).

Of course, if this process of depersonalisation is to work, it is essential that the figures in the book should not be obscured by extraneous presences. If the person of the novelist Flaubert constantly interposes itself between the reader and Félicité, the writer will be much more in evidence than his creations, and identification with the heroine will be impaired. The reader must have the impression that he is alone with the characters, who must appear to have an autonomous existence of their own, and not to be just the puppets of an omniscient author. For these purposes, in the case of someone simple-minded and unsophisticated like Félicité, the writer must suppress any tendency to draw attention to himself by displays of fine writing, of over-subtle analysis, of intellectual abstraction, or of striking imagery. In addition, if we are to see Félicité's happiness as being authentic, and not merely the delusion of a silly old woman, we must see it primarily from the inside: otherwise we may think too much of the deprivations and the sufferings she undergoes, and not enough of the serenity which dominates her inner life. Consequently, Flaubert constantly angles the narration from Félicité's point of view: *Un Cœur simple* is probably more consistently focused on the central character than any other work by Flaubert: hardly ever do we see her through the eyes of someone else – at most when Mme Aubain is struck by the young girl's good will and uncomplaining nature, and when Théodore, after his proposal of marriage, sees her disappearing into the darkness. Apart from such minor instances, we experience the world largely as Félicité herself experiences it. That is to say that much of the tale consists of simple and direct evocations of a concrete reality, firmly set in nineteenth-century rural Normandy. The sentences are short, the grammatical constructions straightforward, the vocabulary everyday, and aphoristic generalisations largely eschewed, so that any sense of dichotomy between author and character is avoided. In particular, Flaubert keeps an extremely tight rein on his natural inclination towards rich and elaborate imagery, which had caused him to say, during work on *Madame Bovary*: 'je suis gêné par le sens métaphorique qui décidément me domine trop. Je suis dévoré de comparaisons, comme on l'est de poux, et je ne passe mon temps qu'à les écraser; mes phrases en grouillent' (27 December, 1852; *1*, XIII, p.275). Here, the avoidance of ornate images is essential if we are to identify with Félicité and forget the man of letters who is writing about her. Hence the comparisons are few, unobtrusive and taken exclusively from Félicité's limited experience of the world. In the 61 pages of a plain text, there are only 24 comparisons, which gives an average density of 0.39 per page (the significance of this figure will become clear when it is compared with the other two tales), and their simplicity is evident: the sea appears 'comme une tache grise' (p.49), mist floats 'comme une écharpe' (p.49), the sea is smooth 'comme un miroir' (p.52), a sail swells 'comme un ballon' (p.53). Only at rare moments of emotional intensity do they go beyond this modest pictorial function. On hearing of Victor's death, Félicité returns to her washing by the riverside: 'le vent agitait la rivière; au fond, de grandes herbes s'y penchaient, comme des chevelures de cadavres flottant dans l'eau' (p.61). Arriving at Honfleur after being struck down by the coachman's whip, 'la misère de son enfance, la déception du premier amour, le départ de son neveu, la mort de Virginie, comme les flots d'une marée, revinrent à la fois, et, lui montant à la gorge, l'étouffaient' (pp.71-72). It is quite exceptional that there should be two consecutive similes in the sentence which leads up to the climax of the story: 'Les mouvements de son cœur se ralentirent un à un, plus vagues chaque fois, plus doux, comme une fontaine s'épuise, comme un écho disparaît' (p.78). This very deliberate restraint in the use of images helps to account for the unpretentious nature of the prose of *Un Cœur simple*, which Flaubert himself described as 'bonhomme' (2 September 1876; *1*, XV, p.489).

Not that Flaubert has forced himself to remain within the narrow bounds of Félicité's limited intelligence and rudimentary powers of expression. By his favourite device of *style indirect libre*, the use of the imperfect tense without indication of who is thinking or speaking, he sets up a deliberate ambiguity, so that he can imperceptibly assist Félicité in the translation of her thoughts and feelings without either overtly stepping outside her or restricting himself to her inarticulateness. Thus it is that, in the description of Félicité's room, he is able to open with this sentence: 'Cet endroit, où elle admettait peu de monde, avait l'air tout à la fois d'une chapelle et d'un bazar, tant il contenait d'objets religieux et de choses hétéroclites' (p.72), in which the point of view is implicitly Félicité's, since few other people ever penetrate into her sanctum, in which the comparisons with a chapel and a bazaar belong firmly to the world with which she is familiar, but where the word 'hétéroclites', no doubt chosen in preference to 'diverses' or 'variées' for its oddity and angularity, is certainly no part of her limited vocabulary. By means such as these, Flaubert induces the reader to see the world through Félicité's eyes, while not hamstringing himself by writing with the incoherence and inexpressiveness which would be all she could manage herself.

This impression of unspoken sympathy with Félicité is enhanced by the way in which the other characters in the story and their attitudes towards her are presented. When Flaubert averred that the tale was 'nullement ironique, mais au contraire très sérieux et très triste', he did not mean that irony was totally absent from it, but rather that, in this one instance, the main character, unlike Emma Bovary or Frédéric Moreau, was not the butt of it. On the other hand, those who come into contact with Félicité are by no means exempt from ironic treatment. The most obvious case is that of M. Bourais, the retired solicitor who looks after Mme Aubain's affairs. With his pedantry, his self-importance, his hypocrisy, his lack of feeling for others, he clearly belongs to the same family of minds as M. Homais, the pharmacist in *Madame Bovary*. Indeed, his name gives the game away, since it is composed of the first syllable of that of Bournisien and the second syllable of that of Homais, those apparently antithetical but in reality symmetrical adversaries in the 1857 novel ('Bou-' or 'Bo-' at the beginning of a proper name is, in Flaubert, an invariable sign of a stupid and negative character, with its overtones of 'bourgeois' and 'bovin'). That Bourais is a pompous nonentity is made apparent by the exaggerated respect which the naïve Félicité feels for him and which inspires in her 'ce trouble où nous jette le spectacle des hommes extraordinaires' (p.48). The list of his qualities is visibly derisory: he 'craignait toujours de se compromettre, respectait infiniment la magistrature, avait des prétentions au latin' (p.48). The scorn for him is overt when he makes fun of Félicité's inability to understand a map: 'il avait un beau sourire de cuistre devant l'ahurissement de Félicité (...) Bourais leva les bras, il éternua, rit énormément: une candeur pareille excitait sa joie' (p.60). But he himself suffers the gross indignity of being regularly laughed at by the parrot: 'La figure de Bourais, sans doute, lui paraissait très drôle. Dès qu'il l'apercevait, il commençait à rire, à rire de toutes ses forces. Les éclats de sa voix bondissaient dans la cour, l'écho les répétait, les voisins se mettaient à leurs fenêtres, riaient aussi; et pour n'être pas vu du perroquet, M. Bourais se coulait le long du mur, en dissimulant son profil avec son chapeau, atteignait la rivière, puis entrait par la porte du jardin; et les regards qu'il envoyait à l'oiseau manquaient de tendresse' (p.68). If Bourais's pretentious bourgeois respectability is thus mocked by the parrot, it is completely destroyed by the revelations about his character which eventually come to light. In *Madame Bovary*, the ascension of his counterpart Homais is irresistible and the novel ends with his apotheosis. Here, on the other hand, this epitome of bourgeois correctness is found to be a swindler, to have a mistress and to be the father of an illegitimate child: in the end, he commits suicide. *Un Cœur simple* thus implicitly turns round the structure of *Madame Bovary*, where the heroine is destroyed and the least sympathetic character triumphs; here the heroine triumphs and the least sympathetic character gets his just deserts.

Mme Aubain is treated less harshly, but it is clear that she is a snobbish and narrow-minded woman. She lives only for the memory of her dead husband and for her two children, and remains, with one momentary exception, totally indifferent to any human feelings her maid may have. When Félicité worries about not having received news of her nephew Victor on the high seas, Mme Aubain is unmoved: ' "Ah! votre neveu!" Et, haussant les épaules, Mme Aubain reprit sa promenade, ce qui voulait dire: "Je n'y pensais pas! Au surplus, je m'en moque! un mousse, un gueux, belle affaire! ... tandis que ma fille... Songez donc! ..." ' (pp.59-60). The only break in this haughty disdain for Félicité occurs when, after Virginie's death, the two women come across her clothes in a wardrobe and sink into each other's arms: 'elles s'étreignirent, satisfaisant leur douleur dans un baiser qui les égalisait' (p.66). But this moment of communion never recurs, 'Mme Aubain n'étant pas d'une nature expansive' (p.66), just as we are told, on her death, that 'Peu d'amis la regrettèrent, ses façons étant d'une hauteur qui éloignait' (p.74).

As for her children, if Virginie has no special attributes and elicits our pity by her premature death, Paul is presented with sardonic mockery as he grows up. He proves incapable of sticking to a job, passes his time in cafés and runs up debts which his mother is obliged to pay. Eventually, a sarcastically grandiloquent passage informs us of his success: 'Après avoir été d'abord clerc de notaire, puis dans le commerce, dans la douane, dans les contributions, et même avoir commencé des démarches pour les eaux et forêts, à trente-six ans, tout à coup, par une inspiration du ciel, il avait découvert sa voie: l'enregistrement!' (p.73). When Mme Aubain dies, he and his wife arrive with indecent haste ('le temps d'accourir de Besançon' (p.74), as an insultingly offhand parenthesis has it) with one idea in their minds, making as much money as possible out of the inheritance, after which they lose no time in returning to Besançon.

Minor characters fare little better. Mme Aubain's uncle, the marquis de Grémanville, an aristocrat ruined by debauchery, affects distinguished manners but drinks too much and tells dirty stories. Victor's mother encourages him to visit Félicité so that he may cadge presents from her – soap, brown sugar, brandy or money. Fellacher, the taxidermist, hangs on to the parrot for months, and, when it arrives, the description of the stuffed bird culminates in a detail of absurd ostentatiousness, since it holds in its beak 'une noix, que l'empailleur par amour du grandiose avait dorée' (p.72). The coach driver, angry when the deaf Félicité fails to move out of his way, cruelly strikes her down with his whip.

Clearly, Flaubert is no more indulgent towards the population of Pont-l'Evêque than he had been, in *Madame Bovary*, towards that of Yonville, and Félicité finds no more true love or companionship among them than Emma had with Charles, Léon, Rodolphe or Homais. To that extent, Flaubert has indeed remained faithful to his vision of the world and has not 'changed his eyes'. But whereas in *Madame Bovary* the central character disappears before the end and the reader is left only with the collapse of Charles, the callous forgetfulness of Léon and Rodolphe, and the triumph of the obnoxious Homais, here the secondary characters are removed from the scene, and the end is wholly dominated by Félicité and her beatific vision. It is true that there is an unspoken irony in that vision itself, since the reader is aware that there is something ridiculous about confusing the Holy Ghost with a moth-eaten and decrepit stuffed parrot. But to see in that, as Brunetière did, only 'dérision', 'rudesse', 'brutalité comique' (2, p.245), is to betray a woeful insensitivity to the resonances and implications of the tale, and to misconstrue, disastrously, the effects Flaubert is seeking to produce. As he wrote about religions to a friend: 'Je n'aime point les philosophes qui n'ont vu là que jonglerie et sottise. J'y découvre, moi, nécessité et instinct; aussi je respecte le nègre baisant son fétiche autant que le catholique aux pieds du Sacré-Cœur' (30 March 1857; *1*, XIII, p.570).

It may have been noted that, despite the angling of the narration from Félicité's point of view, in some of the comments on characters just quoted, it is possible to distinguish the voice of the narrator. It is the narrator, not Félicité, who identifies Bourais's smile as 'un beau sourire de cuistre' (p.60), who attributes the gilding of the nut to the taxidermist's 'amour du grandiose' (p.72), who marks Paul's discovery of his vocation in the Wills and Probate Registry with an ironically admiring exclamation mark. The fact is that in *Un Cœur simple* Flaubert entrusts to the narrator more readily perceptible functions than in anything he had written since *Madame Bovary*, hence a tone which at times verges on the familiar and the casual. Regional terms from Normandy occur: 'godefiches' (p.52), 'banneau' (p.45), 'dégouttelait' (p.61). The farmer is 'le bonhomme Liébard' (p.61), Félicité's one female friend in her latter years is 'la mère Simon' (p.75) or 'la Simonne' (p.76), the abbreviation 'etc.' is used twice (pp.48 and 74). The punctuation is informal, with the dash used more than four times as frequently as in the other two tales taken together: in fact, on his own final manuscript he punctuated the very last sentence with no fewer than six dashes, subsequently formalised as commas in the printed text. Emotive epithets are not excluded: Virginie's clothes, found after her death, are 'ces pauvres objets' (p.66), and the cancerous old man nursed by Félicité is 'le pauvre vieux' (p.67). Additional information is several times slipped in in brackets, as though it was an afterthought. Occasionally the narrator stands back from the diegetic time in which the story is taking place, in order to set something in a wider temporal perspective, as when he explains of the 'bains de mer à Trouville' that 'Dans ce temps-là, ils n'étaient pas fréquentés' (p.50). At other times, he uses the present tense to assure us of the factual accuracy of his statements: in the farm at Geffosses, 'La cour est en pente, la maison dans le milieu, et la mer, au loin, apparaît comme une tache grise' (p.49), and in the convent at Honfleur, 'Il y a dans le jardin une terrasse d'où l'on découvre la Seine' (p.62). The occasional aphorism, overt or disguised, is used to orientate our reactions, as when we are told that 'pour de pareilles âmes le surnaturel est tout simple' (p.63), or when reference is made to 'l'imagination que donnent les vraies tendresses' (p.56). Elsewhere, the narrator appeals to a fund of common knowledge shared with the reader, for instance in alluding to 'ces choses familières dont parle l'Evangile' (pp.54-55), or when he tells us that Félicité mourned Mme Aubain 'comme on ne pleure pas les maîtres' (p.74). At times, he categorises a person's character or behaviour: Théodore exhibits 'couardise' (p.46), Mme Aubain is not 'une personne agréable' (p.43), Félicité is characterised by 'la bonté de son cœur' (p.66). So, although the narrator largely hides behind Félicité and adapts his narration to her habits of mind, and although he avoids sentimentality and commentary, he still shows signs of humanity, which a careful reading detects (especially if one compares this tale to the other two, where the narrator effaces himself almost completely).

Because the narrator of *Un Cœur simple* is not entirely impassive and because the general effect of the story is uplifting rather than depressing, it has sometimes been supposed that there is in it a certain autobiographical self-indulgence which would account for the fact that the emotion in it seems relatively close to the surface and that its tone is noticeably less harsh than that of most of Flaubert's fiction. That there are autobiographical elements in it is undeniable. The farm at Geffosses really existed; it had belonged to the Flaubert family and was one of the properties Flaubert had had to sell to save his niece and her family from bankruptcy. Proper names are in some cases chosen for personal associations. Grémanville is an obvious echo of Crémanville, a distant cousin of Flaubert; la mère David, the innkeeper of l'Agneau d'or, really existed and the Flaubert family frequently visited her establishment. Fellacher was the name of the copyist Flaubert employed in the 1840s, and one of his childhood friends was called Varin. Most remarkable of all is the name Loulou given to the parrot – an oddity in itself since, as is admitted in the story, 'tous les perroquets s'appellent Jacquot' (p.68). But Loulou is the pet-name Flaubert gave to his beloved niece Caroline. It would be impossible to overlook the connection between the old and lonely Félicité doting on her Loulou, and the equally old and lonely Flaubert devoted to his Loulou. Caroline herself was struck by certain resemblances between her uncle and Félicité: 'Qu'on se rappelle seulement de cette scène entre Mme Aubin [*sic*] et sa servante quand elles rangent ensemble les menus objets ayant appartenu à Virginie.

Un grand chapeau de paille noire que portait ma grand'mère éveillait en mon oncle une émotion semblable; il prenait au clou la relique, la considérait en silence, ses yeux s'humectaient, et respectueusement il la replaçait' (*58*, p.xxii). In addition, the place at which Félicité is knocked down by the carriage is the place at which Flaubert had his first epileptic fit in 1844, with some curiously similar details: the middle of the winter, the galloping horses, the awakening covered in blood (Flaubert's doctor brother, who was with him, had bled him when he had his seizure). There is even a place where the coincidence between the feelings of Félicité and those of Flaubert appears unmistakably close. Describing Félicité in her room with the stuffed parrot, he writes: 'Chaque matin, en s'éveillant, elle l'apercevait à la clarté de l'aube, et se rappelait alors les jours disparus, et d'insignifiantes actions jusqu'en leurs moindres détails, sans douleur, pleine de tranquillité' (pp.72-73). This sounds almost like an echo of what he had written about himself in 1872, to Mme Schlesinger, for whom he had at one time harboured intense affection: 'On m'a donné un chien. Je me promène avec lui, en regardant l'effet du soleil sur les feuilles qui jaunissent; et comme un vieux, je rêve sur le passé, car je suis un vieux. L'avenir pour moi n'a plus de rêves, mais les jours d'autrefois se représentent comme baignés dans une vapeur d'or' (*1*, XV, p.169).

But while these common features suggest how closely Flaubert was able to identify with Félicité, the idea that the tale originated in a desire to dwell emotionally on his own past is hardly tenable.[3] Examination of the drafts and plans shows that only gradually did he localise Félicité's accident at the place where he had his fit, that the names of the characters changed frequently and unpredictably, that at one time Geffosses was going to be called 'Beauregard'. Moreover, if one looks back at the earliest germs of the story, one notes that the tale of the woman growing old in loneliness and chastity was to be set in Flanders, and that the *Perroquet* plan has no specific setting at all. In other words, it is probable that the tale took shape in Flaubert's mind independently of those elements which link it most closely with his

[3]Most of the supposed autobiographical elements in the story were picked out and stressed by Gérard-Gailly (*18*), but subsequent commentators, notably Willenbrink (*24*) have shown that he greatly exaggerated their importance.

own experience. But since it had to be given a particular setting, it may then have been natural for him, in keeping with the positive atmosphere he wanted to establish, to think of places which had positive associations for him. Thus he would have decided to locate it in the Pays d'Auge, which he knew well from his childhood (as Caroline remarks: 'Dans les dernières années, mon oncle avait un charme extrême à revivre sa jeunesse', *58*, p.xxii). Once that decision was taken, it was more or less inevitable that names and places which had special resonance for him should crop up at intervals in the story.

Indeed, these meaningful associations are woven in with many others which help to create a recognisable picture of that part of the country in the 1830s, without having any known connection with Flaubert himself. Gérard-Gailly has argued (*18*, p.191) that Mme Aubain's house really existed in Pont-l'Evêque, but if this is so, it is not one which appears to have meant anything special to Flaubert. The names of real places abound – Ecquemauville, les Ecores, Toucques, St Melaine, Hennequeville, Colleville – and many of the surnames are characteristically Norman: some at least he was reminded of when, the floods having subsided, he was at last able to undertake his journey to Pont-l'Evêque and Honfleur in the second half of April 1876; others had no doubt always been familiar to him.

Clearly it was important to Flaubert that *Un Cœur simple* should be firmly situated in an identifiable setting, minutely and precisely observed. Indeed, the actual writing of the story had to be postponed until the weather cleared sufficiently for him to make his journey to the places where he had decided to locate it. Nor was this the only matter on which he felt the need to underpin the tale with verifiable observations. It can hardly be accidental that Flaubert invited their ex-maid Julie, now old and ailing, to come and stay at Croisset while he was writing *Un Cœur simple*: no doubt he wanted to note the mannerisms of someone of Félicité's age and class. Likewise he documented himself on the illnesses and habits of parrots from the *Dictionnaire universel d'histoire naturelle*, from a translation of a German study of parrots and from the director of the Rouen museum. In addition, he borrowed a stuffed parrot from the Natural History Museum and set it on his desk while he was working, 'afin de m'emplir l'âme de perroquet' (*1*, XV, p.478), as he put it. How much the contemplation of Julie and the stuffed parrot may have helped him we do not know, but certainly his account of the parrot's movements and maladies is authenticated from his sources. The last illnesses of Mme Aubain and Félicité too required a sound medical basis, and the symptoms of their pneumonia are described from a treatise by a Dr Grisolle. The customs of religious processions likewise required checking: as a non-churchgoer, Flaubert himself was unfamiliar with such practices. So he borrowed from more pious friends, and at one stage boasted that he had on his desk a selection of missals and prayer-books belonging to his niece, her husband, a member of the local church choir and his own grandmother.

Since Félicité's life is so remote from political events, there was little need for him to bother with relating her existence to historical reality. It is only when the 1830 July Revolution brings a new sub-prefect to Pont-l'Evêque and with him the parrot which is eventually passed on to Félicité that political events impinge decisively on her life (though passing references to the victims of the 1832 cholera epidemic and the presence of Polish refugees in the early 1830s provide further landmarks). Even so, Flaubert took trouble over chronology (a matter on which he was liable to become extremely confused). The only other dates mentioned in the story are those of purely fictitious domestic events: M. Aubain's death in 1809, Victor's departure in 1819, the repainting of the hall in 1825, the collapse of part of the roof in 1827, Mme Aubain's providing the bread for consecration in 1828, the parrot's death in 1835, Mme Aubain's death in 1853, though in his notes he recorded a few other dates. This care over sequential chronology, coupled with the lack of allusion to historical events, serves both to underline the humble remoteness of Félicité's existence, and to punctuate, with matters of exclusively private significance, the monotony of a life in which nothing much ever happens, in which there are no real crises or dramas, in which there is hardly a story to unfold at all.

This aspect of the theme of the work posed considerable problems of narrative art for Flaubert, and one can understand why he should have abandoned his original intention of entitling the work

Histoire d'un Cœur simple, since the amount of actual storytelling is minimal. Indeed, by encapsulating virtually all of Félicité's life in the first section, from which we know that she will spend half a century in the service of Mme Aubain, he removes any sense of suspense from the tale and instead confers on it a curiously static air. In general, writers of short stories have preferred to avoid relating the whole life of a character, illuminating it instead by means of a single salient incident. Flaubert on the other hand has chosen to recount a whole life, and a life which has no single incident to act as a focal point. This means that the work is largely lacking in any forward impulse, save what is imparted by the passage of time. Félicité herself is a passive character who never looks to the future, and there is nothing in the way of a plot which might cause an action to progress. So we find Flaubert using a variety of devices to move his story on. One is purely verbal, making the transition from one paragraph to the next hinge on a single word: 'Et elle refermait la porte. / Elle l'ouvrait avec plaisir devant M. Bourais, ancien avoué' (p.48). Another is the notation of time, often for a repeated action, as near the end of the second section: 'Virginie, dès les premiers jours, se sentit moins faible (...) L'après-midi, on s'en allait (...) Presque toujours on se reposait dans un pré (...) D'autres fois (...) Les jours qu'il faisait trop chaud (...)' (pp.52-53). Yet another is the abrupt juxtaposition of unrelated paragraphs: 'Mme Aubain l'en dissuada. / Un événement considérable surgit' (p.73). Sometimes temporal sequences are given an illusory appearance of logic: 'M. Paul, un jour, eut l'imprudence de lui souffler aux narines la fumée d'un cigare, une autre fois que Mme Lormeau l'agaçait du bout de son ombrelle, il en happa la virole; enfin, il se perdit' (p.69). The succession of 'un jour', 'une autre fois', 'enfin' suggests a causal concatenation which does not exist: the three statements of which the sentence is composed are in fact completely unconnected. At times, the coincidence which enables the tale to continue is overt: le père Colmiche, the old man whom Félicité has been nursing, dies: 'Il mourut: elle fit dire une messe pour le repos de son âme. / Ce jour-là, il lui advint un grand bonheur' (p.67) – the sub-prefect is promoted and leaves the parrot behind with Mme Aubain. Were it not for the sense conferred on Félicité's life by her beatific deathbed vision, the whole tale would seem inconsequential to the point of meaninglessness, like the lives of the characters of *L'Education sentimentale*.

Of course, Flaubert has at the same time distributed throughout the story elements which later prove to have a sense and which do constitute a chain of explanations. This is most noticeably the case with the preparation for the final vision. When she listens to the priest giving scripture lessons to Virginie, she converts all he says into mental pictures: 'elle croyait voir ...' (p.54), and the paragraph leads up to her imagining a bird: 'elle aima plus tendrement les agneaux par amour de l'Agneau, les colombes à cause du Saint-Esprit' (p.55). The stuffed parrot is given a place of honour in her room, already full of religious articles (rosaries, medallions, statues of the Virgin, a holy water stoup) and the almost equally sacred relics of her private cult of memory, and where the chest of drawers is covered with a sheet 'comme un autel' (p.72). It is further sanctified by its resemblance to the gaudily coloured 'image d'Epinal' portraying the baptism of Christ. There is even a sentence which Flaubert's friends begged him to excise, on the grounds that it was over-subtle for Félicité: 'Le Père, pour s'énoncer, n'avait pu choisir une colombe, puisque ces bêtes-là n'ont pas de voix, mais plutôt un des ancêtres de Loulou' (p.73). According to Zola, 'Flaubert parut très ému, il nous promit d'examiner le cas, il s'agissait simplement de couper la phrase, mais il ne le fit pas, il aurait cru l'œuvre détraquée' (*56*, p.216). The reason for his obstinacy is no doubt that this is not just one more casual detail, intended to reinforce 'l'effet de réel' and which could have been sacrificed without damage to the whole (like certain descriptive passages which Flaubert ruthlessly removed from the drafts), but one of the important links that establish the plausibility of the concluding vision. So it is that, when she is praying, Félicité's eyes stray from the 'image d'Epinal' to the parrot itself, until, eventually, 'elle ... contracta l'habitude idolâtre de dire ses oraisons agenouillée devant le perroquet' (pp.74-75), with the reflection of the sun bringing forth an apparently celestial ray from his glass eye. The reader is thus gradually conditioned to finding wholly natural the final identification of the parrot and the Holy Ghost welcoming her into heaven.

One or two of the earlier episodes are preceded by similarly unobtrusive motivating details. Virginie's death is not a surprise because the incident with the bull gives her 'une affection nerveuse' (p.50), for which the doctor prescribes sea-bathing; a little later, 'Virginie toussait' (p.54); her tears on leaving for her convent-school denote a delicate temperament; the nuns notice that excitement exhausts her and she has to give up her piano lessons; then she grows weaker with palpitations, fever and a hectic complexion: after which she falls ill and dies. But on the whole, the few episodes there are remain detached and isolated (her brief affair with the faithless Théodore, Victor's departure and death, Loulou's momentary disappearance). Characters vanish – Théodore marries, Virginie, Victor, Mme Aubain, Bourais, Liébard, Grémanville all die, Paul goes to live at the other end of France; only Félicité is there from beginning to end. So the rhythm of the story is irregular and lacunary, with many blank periods: 'des années s'écoulèrent ...' (p.65), 'Trois ans plus tard ...' (p.69), 'Bien des années se passèrent ...' (p.75), contrasting with passages where short periods are evoked in detail: the stay in Trouville, Virginie's death, and so forth. But one of Flaubert's great skills in this constant changing of the distance of focus has been to avoid according excessive prominence to the scenes of close-up – the escape from the bull is the one episode which might properly be called dramatic, but nothing leads up to it ('quand l'herbage suivant fut traversé, un beuglement formidable s'éleva', p.49) and its consequences, apart from its effect on Virginie's health, are evoked in three lines, then forgotten: 'Cet événement, pendant bien des années, fut un sujet de conversation à Pont-l'Evêque. Félicité n'en tira aucun orgueil, ne se doutant même pas qu'elle eût rien fait d'héroïque' (p.50).

One way in which Flaubert avoids involving the reader too deeply in individual episodes is by a drastic limitation of the amount of dialogue they contain. One of his principles as a novelist was to 'réserver le style direct pour les *scènes* principales' (15 January 1870; *1*, XIV, p.545), and since in *Un Cœur simple* there is so little 'style direct', that is to say directly reported speech, the reader is less likely to be tempted into thinking that particular scenes have special significance. A rough calculation suggests that no more than about 3% of the text consists of direct speech, whereas the average over the mature novels is nearer 20% for those set in modern times. Not only that, Flaubert, who was eternally mistrustful of the capacity of language for the authentic expression of emotion, has taken care to ensure that a large proportion of the direct speech is, as near as makes no difference, meaningless. Grémanville's mechanical repetition of 'feu mon père' (p.48), Mme Aubain's disdainful 'Ah! votre neveu!' (p.59), Théodore's hypocritical 'Mais non, je vous jure!' (p.46), the callous comment of the doctor on Victor's death in the tropics 'Bon! encore un!' (p.62), Dr Poupart's automatic reassurance that all is not lost in Virginie's last illness 'Pas encore!' (p.62), Félicité's own desperate 'Pauvre petit gars! Pauvre petit gars!' (p.61) on hearing of Victor's death – all these phrases are in themselves empty clichés, something emphasised by the fact that the rare snatches of dialogue in the tale never extend beyond two or three lines. It goes without saying that the parrot's mouthing of phrases imitated with no sense of their meaning mirrors this inadequacy of human language: 'Charmant garçon! Serviteur, monsieur! Je vous salue, Marie!' (p.68), 'Félicité! la porte! la porte!' (p.70). Of course, Flaubert accepts that expressing oneself in clichés or set formulas does not always imply lack of genuine emotion, as he makes clear when he writes that, in their 'conversations', the parrot keeps rattling off 'les trois phrases de son répertoire' and that Félicité responds by 'des mots sans plus de suite, mais où son cœur s'épanchait' (p.70). But real communication through language hardly exists in *Un Cœur simple*, and when Mme Aubain says to her maid: 'Mon Dieu! comme vous êtes bête!' and the deaf Félicité answers: 'Oui, Madame' (p.70), that is only the most obvious instance of a failure of language as a true link between human beings. It is naturally a deliberate choice on Flaubert's part that Félicité's pet should be a parrot, rather than a cat, a dog or a canary: not only do the bright colours of its plumage lead to the confusion with the Holy Ghost as depicted on the 'image d'Epinal', but the parrot's nonsensical chatter, with Félicité's loss of hearing, points to one of the underlying themes of the work.

By keeping dialogue to a minimum, by refusing to bring individual scenes (except Félicité's death) into too detailed close-up, Flaubert is resisting certain temptations to which, as a novelist rather than a short-story writer, he must have been subjected. If one examines the drafts for the tale, it is apparent that Flaubert was constantly fighting against the tendency to expand his account of events, characters and places as a novelist would do. The genesis of the tale is a constant process of expansion and reduction. At various stages, he introduced more secondary characters, developed his portraits of Dr Poupart, Paul and Bourais, was much fuller in his descriptions and his explanations of actions, and allowed himself much more freedom to comment and express opinions. But, as he neared the final text, a rigorous pruning pared the tale down to its present succinctness. As he wrote to his niece, 'dans le commencement, je m'étais emballé dans trop de descriptions. J'en enlève de charmantes: la littérature est l'art des sacrifices' (8 July 1876; *1*, XV, p.464). So it is that the descriptions, which comprise a large part of the story, in accordance with Félicité's direct, physical and unintellectual response to her surroundings, are hardly ever exhaustive, except for Félicité's room (where we have to see how the stuffed parrot fits into her few basic possessions and her collection of pious relics), and the final Corpus Christi procession (where it is essential to create a special effect of magnificence and to motivate the final vision). Otherwise the visits to the seaside at Trouville or the farm at Geffosses, like the fair at Colleville where she meets Théodore or the harbour at Honfleur when Victor sets sail, are evoked only by a few characteristic details, chosen among the many Flaubert visualised and the rest of which the reader is incited to supply for himself. Likewise with the characters: we hear twice of friends of Mme Aubain, referred to as '*ces* demoiselles Rochefeuille' (pp.56 and 68), about whom we learn nothing more, but the repeated demonstrative hints at a whole special atmosphere about them. By such touches, Flaubert convinces us that *Un Cœur simple* is not that self-contained, artificially isolated segment which short stories (even some of the best of them) often suggest, but rather part of a whole living and moving world.

Un Cœur simple is thus unique among short stories, as it is unique in Flaubert's work. Its contained and unsentimental emotion, its remarkable combination of consolation and clearsightedness, its apparently simple and direct appeal, its suggestion of a viable way of life in a grim and unforgiving world make it, for many readers, one of the highest peaks of Flaubert's achievement.

3. La Légende de Saint Julien l'Hospitalier

Whereas *Un Coeur simple* is (so far as is known) an entirely invented story, whatever accretions it may have acquired from documentation or Flaubert's own experience, *La Légende de Saint Julien l'Hospitalier* is a wholly different case. The story of St Julian is a genuine medieval hagiographical legend, which Flaubert knew in various forms and to the general outlines of which he obviously intended to keep (there is no question of a deliberate deformation of the legend such as one finds in sceptical retellings of Saints' lives by, for instance, Anatole France). It is thus essential to begin by looking at the legend as Flaubert knew it, before attempting to assess what he made of it.

Certain elements are common to all the old versions of the legend. When out hunting, Julian encountered a stag, which predicted that he would kill his parents. Because of this, he left home and travelled widely, eventually marrying and settling in a distant land. His parents set off in search of him and finally reached his castle, while he was absent. His wife received them with kindness and gave them her own bed. Julian returned in the night and, believing that his wife was in bed with another man, killed them both. He and his wife then went away and did penance by setting up as ferrymen and devoting themselves to the welfare of travellers. In the end, God accepted their penance, and Julian was recognised as a saint.

It is probable that Flaubert first came across the legend as it appears on a stained-glass window in Rouen cathedral, to which he makes explicit reference in the last sentence of the story. But he seems also to have associated the story with the church at Caudebec-en-Caux, near Rouen, where there is a statue of another, different St Julian, as well as part of a window depicting St Eustace or St Hubert, both of whom also encountered a talking stag. Flaubert visited this church in 1835, in the company of his art-master, Eustache-Hyacinthe Langlois, the author of an *Essai historique et descriptif sur la peinture sur verre ancienne et moderne*, published in 1832, which included a long account of the Rouen window and a line drawing of it by his daughter. It may well be that on that occasion, prompted by the sight of the representation of the other St Julian and the window showing the talking stag, Langlois drew his young friend's attention to the story of Julian on the window in Rouen. That would explain why Flaubert's friend Maxime Du Camp should have averred in his *Souvenirs littéraires*, alluding to their joint explorations of the Normandy countryside around 1846: 'C'est dans une de ces excursions que Flaubert, regardant, je crois, les vitraux de l'église de Caudebec, conçut l'idée de son conte de *Saint Julien l'Hospitalier*' (*57*, I, p.237).

It was some ten years later that Flaubert made his first attempt to put this intention into practice. In 1856, having finished *Madame Bovary* and wanting to fill in time before returning to a new version of *La Tentation de Saint Antoine*, abandoned after the mauling it had received when he read it to Du Camp and Louis Bouilhet in 1849, he produced a plan for his legend and took notes on various books on hunting and life in the Middle Ages. The plan drafted at that time outlines the story very much as he eventually wrote it, but a letter to Bouilhet suggests that then he envisaged the work in a somewhat different and perhaps less sombre spirit: 'Je lis des bouquins sur la vie domestique au moyen âge et la vénerie. Je trouve des détails superbes et neufs. Que dis-tu "d'un pâté de hérissons et d'une froumentée d'écureuils"? (...) J'ai relu *Pécopin*, je n'ai aucune peur de la ressemblance' (1 June 1856; *1*, XIII, p.522). The mention of picturesque details and of Hugo's *Légende du Beau Pécopin et de la Belle Bauldour*, an exuberantly fantastic account of a spectral hunt inserted in the travel-book *Le Rhin*, hints at a freer and less grave treatment of the legend than we eventually find. But while he went quite a long way in preparing his tale in 1856, he does not appear to have begun writing, nor did the notes he took then supply any material for the final composition.

But at least that planning stood him in good stead when, in the circumstances related in my Introduction, he was casting around for some brief piece he could write without involving himself in the agony of creating something out of nothing. Exactly how many versions of the legend he consulted is uncertain. Obviously he knew the rendering by Langlois, which does not adhere strictly to the Rouen window, the interpretation of which is in places obscure and dubious; to make his account coherent, Langlois also had recourse to the life of Julian as recounted by the Bollandists. Flaubert can hardly have liked the declamatory, sentimental and moralising style adopted by Langlois, but he granted it the virtue of clarity in narration ('elle est bien racontée' he told his niece Caroline: 30 September 1875, *1*, XV, p.409). He knew too the concise account in Jacopus da Voragine's *Legenda Aurea*, of which he owned a French translation, also recommended to Caroline. And at some stage, probably in 1856 but perhaps not until 1875, he also read a transcription in modern French of a medieval manuscript in the Municipal Library at Alençon, published in the *Mémoires de la Société des Antiquaires de l'Ouest* by G.-F.-G. Lecointre-Dupont. The idea, current a few years ago, that he went so far as to consult an unpublished medieval manuscript in the Bibliothèque Nationale has now been exploded:[4] it is highly unlikely he could have known of its existence and he did not possess the palaeographic skills necessary to decipher it. In fact, some of the things which most impressed him in Langlois's account or in Lecointre-Dupont's version (which, far from being a rigorous transcription, is rendered with a good deal of freedom and supplementation from other sources) are not genuinely medieval at all, but part of the nineteenth-century glosses on the legend, notably some of the descriptive passages in which he unmistakably echoes his recent predecessors, and in his attempt to put a credible psychological construction on Julian's life and actions, which is irrelevant to the intentions of the medieval hagiographers.

[4] The idea that Flaubert had read the medieval manuscript was first aired by Miss S. Smith in an M.A. thesis for the University of Manchester in 1944; it was then given publicity in an article by E. Vinaver (*35*), in C. Duckworth's edition (*4*) and in R. Baldick's 1961 Penguin translation. I challenged it in 1965 (*37*), but my case was not accepted by either Duckworth (*38*) or Vinaver (*40*). There matters rested until the publication of the book by B.F. Bart and R.F. Cook (*44*); their careful examination of all the evidence seems to settle the question once and for all: Flaubert did not consult a medieval manuscript but only Lecointre-Dupont's unfaithful transcription of one.

When he returned to the story at Concarneau in 1875, he had none of his notes and papers with him, and once he had become immersed in composition, rapidly grew impatient to have access to books, and as soon as he returned to Paris, began voraciously to read modern editions of medieval treatises on venery and falconry, which provided him with numerous names of species, details of hunting techniques and the like, and no doubt took a closer look at Lecointre-Dupont, which leaves many traces on the language of the tale, most notably in the last section. But while his correspondence regularly informs us of the progress of composition, it contains few if any hints of his intentions in writing the tale comparable to those we find for *Un Cœur simple* and *Hérodias*. The allusions that do occur are so obviously mocking as to be of little value as clues: it is a 'petite historiette (religioso-pohétique [s.c] et moyenâgeusement rococo)' (5 January 1875; *1*, XV, p.432) or an 'œuvre édifiante, qui me fera passer pour "tourner au cléricalisme" ' (12 February 1876; *1*, XV, p.436).

But one thing is clear throughout: Flaubert wants the reader to have in mind the stained-glass window in Rouen cathedral. The 1856 plan concludes with a sentence, already fully formed, which will survive almost unchanged into the published text over twenty years later: 'Et voilà la légende de St Julien l'hospitalier telle qu'elle est racontée sur les vitraux de la cath[édrale] de ma ville natale' (*1*, IV, pp.472-73). Indeed, when in 1879 there was some question of the publisher Charpentier bringing out a separate luxury edition of *Saint Julien*, Flaubert wanted to include in it a reproduction of the window. Edmond de Goncourt records thus his conversation with Charpentier:

FLAUBERT - Eh bien, Charpentier, faites-vous mon SAINT-JULIEN?
CHARPENTIER - Mais oui ... vous tenez toujours à ce vitrail de la
            cathédrale de Rouen, qui - c'est vous qui le dites - n'a aucun
            rapport avec votre livre?
FLAUBERT - Oui, parfaitement, et c'est bien à cause de cela. (...)
- Mais, lui crie-t-on, avec votre vitrail seul, la publication n'a aucune
            chance de succès! Vous en vendrez vingt exemplaires... Puis,
            pourquoi vous butez-vous à une chose que vous-même
            reconnaissez être absurde?
FLAUBERT - avec un geste à la Frédérick Lemaître. - C'est absolument
            pour épater le bourgeois! (*60*, III, p.27)

This exchange is somewhat clarified by the letter Flaubert had sent to Charpentier a few months earlier: 'Je désirais mettre à la suite de *Saint Julien* le vitrail de la cathédrale de Rouen. Il s'agissait de colorier la planche qui se trouve dans le livre de Langlois, rien de plus. Et cette illustration me plaisait précisément parce que ce n'était pas une illustration, mais un document historique. En comparant l'image au texte on se serait dit: "Je n'y comprends rien. Comment a-t-il tiré ceci de cela?" ' (16 February 1879; *1*, XVI, p.146).

There is a certain mischievousness in these declarations. Flaubert was fiercely opposed to having any of his novels illustrated, on the ground that illustrations would interfere with the mental images each reader would form of the events and characters evoked. But when he postulates the derivation of his *Légende* from the Rouen window while at the same time averring that the two were unrelated, he is in one sense misleading the reader, who would indeed be unable to work out how he had 'tiré ceci de cela', since the window is not one of the prime direct sources of his treatment, other than through Langlois's rather idiosyncratic interpretation of it. But if laying this false trail does smack of 'épater le bourgeois', it also has a serious function akin to that of the last sentence. This is to suggest a perfectly valid analogy between his tale and the art of medieval stained glass. We are not being invited to look directly at the life of the Middle Ages, as in *Salammbô* we look directly at Carthage or in *Un Cœur simple* at early nineteenth-century Normandy. Flaubert's friend Hippolyte Taine summed this up perfectly when he wrote to congratulate the writer: 'Julien est très vrai, mais c'est le monde *imaginé* par le moyen âge, et non le moyen âge lui-meme; ce que vous souhaitiez, puisque vous vouliez produire l'effet d'un vitrail; cet effet y est; la poursuite de Julien par les bêtes, le lépreux, tout du pur idéal de l'an 1200' (4 May 1877; *2*, p.227).

There are all sorts of ways in which Flaubert produces this effect. One lies in the very title, which informs us in advance that we are dealing with a legend, not with reality, and that the legend is that of a saint. Hence we know that in the end Julien will attain sainthood: to that extent, all is predetermined, and suspense lies only in the tortuous route which leads to this conclusion. As with a stained-glass window, one can thus take everything in at once, even if one then follows through the story panel by panel. Secondly, sainthood and the supernatural are taken for granted: there is no questioning of divine intervention in the events recounted: 'A force de prier Dieu, il lui vint un fils' (p.80), we are told in terms which brook no doubt, and at the end, Julien's ascent into heaven with Christ is presented as a fact, with none of the reticence introduced into the end of *Un Cœur simple* by the significant 'elle crut voir'. Thirdly, the narration makes little or no attempt to convince us that we are dealing with a world as real as that of Pont-l'Evêque, and nearly all the detail which, by its very gratuitousness, leads to 'l'effet de réel' is omitted. We do not know what country or what century we are in; we do not know Julien's surname or the name of his wife; the descriptions of his parents' castle or the palace he lives in later consist only of a few characteristic features. We are told nothing of Julien's appearance, and that of his parents and his wife is evoked in conventional terms which do not allow us to visualise them as individuals. Lastly, the style is finely angled so as to give it an almost imperceptible medieval colouring and remove it, however slightly, from the naturalness of modern French. This is done in part by the use of archaic vocabulary, sometimes terms designating things which have since disappeared ('braquemarts' (p.80), 'douves' (p.79), 'échauguette' (p.80), 'manants' (p.80)), sometimes archaic words preferred to their modern equivalents ('maîtres mires' (p.90) not 'médecins', 'nefs' (p.83) not 'navires', 'occis' (p.88) not 'tués'). Sometimes words still current are employed in a vanished sense ('erreurs' (p.83) for wanderings, 'drapeaux' (p.104) for pieces of cloth). Other words are selected from rare and elevated reaches of the language ('encadrure' (p.100), 'rai' (p.81), 'enfonçures' (p.88), 'camérières' (p.85). 'ensevelissement' (p.101)): others still are introduced into contexts far removed from their normal connotations: it is 'une voix', not 'un cri', which is 'longuement poussée' (p.100), the caliph maltreats his captive 'afin d'en extirper des trésors' (p.92), a phrase Flaubert maintained despite the pertinent objection of a friend that 'extorquer' would be more correct (2, p.226). In places, too, the syntax is deliberately, if discreetly, stilted ('s'enfuyant d'horreur' (p.100), 'C'est lui, et pas un autre, qui assomma la guivre de Milan et le dragon d'Oberbirbach' (p.92), 'Et tombait dans un assoupissement où les visions funèbres continuaient' (p.105) with elision of the pronoun subject, or somewhat unexpected inversions: 'et, çà et là, parurent entre les branches quantité de larges étincelles' (p.98)). The mild feeling of strangeness is reinforced by the long lists of unfamiliar terms, notably the catalogues of exotic species of hunting-dogs or of birds of prey.

In these catalogues, Flaubert is plainly not much concerned with functional precision. If in the final text, Julien's favourite falcon is a white 'tartaret de Scythie' (p.85), he opts for that origin only after having tried out 'Norvège', 'Islande' and 'Scandinavie', and though his sources told him that the 'tiercelet' originates in Armenia, he prefers to talk of 'des tiercelets du Caucase' (p.85). In the second hunt, if many of the animals are unexceptionally European – bulls, squirrels, owls, partridges – others are of totally disparate origin – panthers, hyenas, apes, parrots, bears. Obviously, in all this Flaubert is interested in sonority and exoticism rather than in zoological plausibility: neither he nor his readers care much about the precise attributes and specialities of the various species of hunting-dogs he lists. We marvel at their strangeness, as we would marvel at the strangeness of the exhibits in some vast imaginary museum.

Something similar is visible in Flaubert's use of proper names in *Saint Julien*. As we have seen, many proper names – of people and countries – are omitted. Those which do appear tend to be fabulous or so distant in time that they are surrounded by an aura of fable – Occitanie, les Garamantes, Oberbirbach. Where clearly identifiable places are named, they tend to be associated with legendary features that remove them from a realistic context: thus, if we hear of Milan, it is only in connection with an imaginary creature, the 'guivre' (originally a heraldic beast; p.92). The use of capital letters for certain figures – l'Ermite, le Lépreux – marks them out as mythical beings.

All these devices combine to keep the reader at arm's length from the events narrated and the people who participate in them. But it is important to note that Flaubert has steered a careful course between two traps which his immediate predecessors had not avoided. One is that exemplified by Langlois, whose declamatory rhetoric opens up an uncomfortable gap between the language and what it relates: one is very conscious of the discrepancy between an unmistakably modern style and the medieval legend recounted. At the other extreme, Lecointre-Dupont produces a clumsy and artificial pastiche of medieval French, as here: 'Dame, répond le comte, ne savez mie de quoi voulez vous entremettre. Jamais ne pourriez aller ainsi deschause comme il convient de faire, et ne feriez que m'arrêter' (*44*, p.144). Flaubert uses his archaisms with infinitely more discretion: the spelling is never archaic; archaisms are banished from direct speech; and where they do occur, they never draw attention to themselves. In catalogues, mythic and exotic animals tend only to appear after we have met more familiar species. So, while the reader cannot ever feel completely at home in the linguistic world of *Saint Julien*, he is never shocked or affronted by too insistent departures from the norm.

The references to divine intervention in Julien's life are likewise handled with unobtrusive skill. With the prophecies made to Julien's father and mother, the use of point of view and 'style indirect libre' means that one cannot wholly exclude the possibility of hallucination, and it has been argued, by A.E. Pilkington (*42*, p.273), that 'for each supernatural event in *Saint Julien* there is left open the possibility of a rational explanation in terms of psychology', rather in the manner of Mérimée's *La Vénus d'Ille*. So even if the reader is hardly invited to explain away the supernatural occurrences, he is equally not forced to suspend his critical faculty. There are from time to time reminders that God governs all that is happening: 'A force de prier Dieu, il lui vint un fils' (p.80), which may be the assumed medieval narrator's gloss on a natural event, as may be the assertion that it was 'grâce à la faveur divine' (p.91) that Julien always escaped death in his martial exploits. 'Elle entendit les voix des anges' (p.81), 'le respectant comme marqué de Dieu' (p.82) are perhaps wishful thinking on the part of Julien's parents. Only rarely does Julien reflect on the problem of how he can be held responsible for a crime which divine predestination compelled him to commit: 'Sa prédiction l'obsédait, il se débattait contre elle. "Non! non! non! je ne peux pas les tuer!" puis il songeait: "Si je le voulais pourtant?..." et il avait peur que le Diable ne lui en inspirât l'envie' (p.90), and 'Il ne se révoltait pas contre Dieu qui lui avait infligé cette action, et pourtant se désespérait de l'avoir pu commettre' (p.103). The rarity of such reflections means that we are scarcely induced to worry about the complexities of free will, predestination and morality, while we are kept aware that there is more than a purely human dimension to the action.

The use of symbols and distant allusions to other legends and myths also contributes to this atmosphere. Twice Julien is presented in the attitude of the crucifixion: once in the first hunt when he falls on the corpse of the wild goat he has just killed and remains 'la face au-dessus de l'abîme et les deux bras écartés' (p.87) and again, after the parricide, when he appears dressed as a monk, 'à plat ventre au milieu du portail, les bras en croix, et le front dans la poussière' (p.101). Then there is an apparent reference to the legends of St Eustace and St Hubert, who both met a miraculous stag with a cross between its antlers, when Julien shoots his last arrow at the great stag: 'Elle l'atteignit au front, et y resta plantée' (p.89). In the Leper episode, it is impossible not to think of the St Christopher legend.

The legend presents clear analogies with the Greek myth of Oedipus. The Delphic oracle predicted to Laios king of Thebes that his son Oedipus would kill him and marry his mother, so the boy was abandoned in the mountains. But he was saved and brought up by shepherds: many years later, on his way to Delphi to try to discover the secret of his birth, he quarrelled with an unknown old man whom he killed but who was in fact his father. He then became king and married the widow of Laios, thus fulfilling the prophecy. On realising his crimes, he put out his eyes. This archetypal myth gave rise to two tragedies by Sophocles and modern versions by Dryden, Corneille, Voltaire, Gide and Cocteau, as well as to the Oedipus complex identified by Freud.

But if in all this, Flaubert remains faithful to the spirit of the legend and of medieval stained glass, he also injects into his tale something which is foreign to these models. That is his insistence on the psychological motivation of Julian's actions. None of his sources has much to say about Julien's boyhood, but Flaubert relates it in detail, largely in order to introduce the meticulous gradation of the stages in Julien's delight in slaughter (which in itself is his own addition to the story): first there is the killing of the mouse in the chapel, then the shooting down of little birds, next the strangling of the wounded pigeon, with its unmistakable overtones of sexual pleasure ('les convulsions de l'oiseau faisaient battre son cœur, l'emplissaient d'une volupté sauvage et tumultueuse. Au dernier raidissement, il se sentit défaillir', p.84), the preoccupation with hunting, the massacre of the animals in the first hunt; then, after the period of anxious avoidance of hunting, the second frustrating hunt in which the animals, mysteriously invulnerable, mock him and reduce him to a state of murderous exasperation: 'Sa soif de carnage le reprenait, les bêtes manquant, il aurait voulu massacrer des hommes' (p.99). The murder of his parents is thus not just the sudden result of an understandable mistake, but the culmination of a long process of intensifying pleasure in killing. In this process, there are moments when Julien's feelings are depicted with a minuteness which brings him into close-up as a real human being: 'Julien avait traversé le parc, et il marchait dans la forêt d'un pas nerveux, jouissant de la mollesse du gazon et de la douceur de l'air. Les ombres des arbres s'étendaient sur la mousse. Quelquefois la lune faisait des taches blanches dans les clairières, et il hésitait à s'avancer, croyant apercevoir une flaque d'eau, ou bien la surface des mares tranquilles se confondait avec la couleur de l'herbe' (p.97).

In thus seeking to give a coherent psychological structure to the hagiographical legend, Flaubert is following a tendency common in nineteenth-century exegesis of mythology, as practised in their academic studies by a number of his friends such as Ernest Renan and Alfred Maury. That in so doing he was departing from the tradition in which he wanted to place himself seems not to have worried him, and it is true that he manages the transitions with such artistry that the reader may well not notice the disparity. The desire for psychological plausibility is not the only respect in which Flaubert deviates from his medieval exemplars, since he also makes some alterations to the details of the story while leaving its basic outlines intact. One of the most significant is the elimination of Julien's wife from the later stages of the tale. In the legendary versions, she accepts a share of the guilt for the parricide, accompanies her husband in his penance, and is eventually pardoned with him. But Flaubert, determined to concentrate our attention on Julien, presumably regards the wife as an intrusive irrelevance, so that, in his tale, she is bidden to remain behind when Julien departs and is never mentioned again. Indeed, by refusing her a name, he has already reduced her status to that of an adjunct to Julien, as he has reduced Julien's father to his warlike and hunting propensities and his mother to her piety, so that they all only exist in so far as they impinge on Julien's fate. The other major divergence from the medieval tradition lies in making the whole tale hinge on hunting. Hunting is not absent from the medieval texts, since it is while Julien is out hunting that the stag predicts the murders and since in some versions, including Lecointre-Dupont's, he is away hunting when his parents arrive. But making the obsession with hunting the pivot of the whole legend is Flaubert's own idea, and it is only in his version that Julien kills the stag after the prophecy: in all the texts he knew, Julien flees straight away. Clearly, these changes are designed to focus our attention more rigorously on Julien and to confer on his fate a psychological necessity it did not otherwise have.

The conjunction of a certain psychological determinism and the idea of divine will and prescience (however uneasily they may, on reflection, sit together) does at least conduce to an impression of inevitability, and this naturally leads to a very different mode of narration from that found in *Un Cœur simple*. Here there is no question of a lacunary account moving forward by fits and starts. On the contrary, in *Saint Julien* the structure is very tightly knit, and the tale depends on a network of visible links and symmetries. One underlying symmetry is established in the opening pages: the contrast between the martial and hunting world of the father and the gentle pious world of the mother, which founds not only the murderer/saint dichotomy in Julien's character but also the various stages of his development, and is of course reflected in the twin apparitions of the Hermit and the Gipsy. Then we have the symmetrical antithesis of the two hunts: the one in which Julien kills all the animals with unaccountable ease, and the other in which the animals are inexplicably invulnerable and turn on him. There are two sets of wanderings on which Julien embarks: the warlike exploits when he leaves home and the penitential travels after the murders. There are two main dwellings for Julien, his parents'

castle and the palace he inhabits with his wife – always meant to form
a complementary contrast ('le bien différencier du paternel', Flaubert
notes in 1856; *1*, IV, p.472). Often these symmetries have a triple form:
three chapters, three departures of Julien, three summonses from the
Leper, three ritual demands, even three stages in the idea of killing
(killing animals, killing one's parents, then killing oneself – though
Julien draws back from this at the last minute). These broader
symmetries are underpinned by a variety of linked, quasi-symbolic
details. At the windows of the parents' castle are basil and heliotrope,
which in the medieval language of flowers stood for cruel rage and
divine inspiration respectively. The Gipsy has 'prunelles
flamboyantes' (p.81), the stag has 'les yeux flamboyants' (p.89),
Julien, looking at his father's corpse, sees 'une prunelle éteinte qui le
brûla comme du feu' (p.101), and the Leper has 'les deux yeux plus
rouges que des charbons' (p.105). When the stag's prediction of
parricide is fulfilled, Julien hears again 'le bramement du grand cerf
noir' (p.100). As the stag makes its prophecy, 'une cloche au loin
tintait' (p.89), and when the Leper calls to Julien, 'cette voix ... avait
l'intonation d'une cloche d'église' (p.105). Like the fiery eyes the
beard recurs: the Gipsy has a 'barbe tressée' (p.81), the stag a 'barbe
blanche' (p.89) and at his death the father a 'grande barbe' (p.96).

Images and colours echo these connections. One series of
images continues the theme of religion inaugurated by the mother's
piety: the cobblestones of the courtyard are clean 'comme le dallage
d'une église' (p.79), the archer falls asleep 'comme un moine' (p.80),
the baby Julien 'ressemblait à un petit Jésus' (p.82), the father
'ressemblait à une statue d'église' (p.96), Julien imagines himself in
the midst of the animals 'comme notre père Adam' (p.94). But a
corresponding series of images of royalty relates to the father's side:
trees form 'comme un arc de triomphe' (p.87), the chapel is
'somptueuse comme l'oratoire d'un roi' (p.80), the great stag is
solemn 'comme un patriarche et comme un justicier' (p.89), in the
Leper's attitude there is 'comme une majesté de roi' (p.105). Likewise
colours are used, not only to evoke the rich tones of a stained-glass
window, but to give oblique expression to thematic material. On the
one hand, we have the white of innocence: Julien's mother is 'très

blanche' (p.80), the mouse he kills is white, the hind is light-coloured 'comme les feuilles mortes' (p.89), in old age his mother's hair resembles 'des plaques de neige' (p.96), the harmless arrows in the second hunt land 'comme des papillons blancs' (p.98). On the other hand is the red of crime and bloodshed; over his mother's bed hangs 'un os de martyr dans un cadre d'escarboucles' (p.81), there are numerous mentions of blood and the fire of eyes; after the massacre of the animals 'le ciel était rouge comme une nappe de sang' (p.89). In the scene of the parricide, Flaubert lavishly spreads red on white: the blood of his parents, shed by Julien, is everywhere: 'Des éclaboussures et des flaques de sang s'étalaient au milieu de leur peau blanche, sur les draps du lit, par terre, le long d'un christ d'ivoire suspendu dans l'alcôve' (p.100). The sinister implications of black set off these brighter colours: the spaniels have black coats, during the first hunt the sky is black, one of his victims is 'un castor à museau noir' (p.87), the great stag is black, it is during the night that Julien scales the walls of besieged cities, the parricide takes place in darkness, when the Leper summons him 'les ténèbres étaient profondes' (p.105), and as he rows back through the storm, the water is 'plus noire que de l'encre' (p.106).

Even apparently insignificant details may prove to have unexpected overtones. In the story as a whole, there is an immense catalogue of animals, with over a hundred species mentioned by name – ordinary domestic animals, exotic beasts, mammals, fish and reptiles, even mythical and prehistoric creatures, dragon, aurochs, the 'guivre de Milan' (p.92). But they are carefully differentiated in the two antithetical hunts, with in the first nearly all of them inoffensive, while in the second, far more of them are dangerous – a bull, a snake, a wolf, hyenas and so forth. But only one animal figures in both enumerations, the fox. As P.-M. de Biasi has pointed out (48), it is hard to believe this is an accident, especially when one remembers that elsewhere in the tale, fox fur is the distinguishing mark of the father: the first mention of him shows him 'toujours enveloppé d'une pelisse de renard' (p.80), and at the very end, Julien recalls him as 'un vieillard couvert de fourrures' (p.105). The persistence of these references to the fox/father confirms what is already suggested by the theme of the burning eyes associated with the various father figures, namely, that relations with the father, and in particular guilt feelings towards him, are at the core of the story. 'Sans le savoir, ce que désire Julien, c'est tuer le père-renard' (*48*, p.270).

Clearly, the network of symbols, metonymy and synecdoche is so dense that we are necessarily invited to attempt a hermeneutic reading of the tale in a way which would hardly be possible with the other two. The impression that these thematic recalls, symmetries and oppositions are deliberately organised so as to produce a meaningful structure is enhanced by the care with which, on the level of style, the rhythms of the language are so arranged as to convey a sense of plenitude and of rightness. In *Un Cœur simple* the rhythms are irregular and the movement fitful: Saint Julien works in a completely different way. It is well known that Flaubert was fond of ternary structures (though it is easy to exaggerate this). But in *Saint Julien* there can be no doubting the predominance of ternary rhythms, especially those which create an expectation by presenting two balancing elements, which are then completed by a longer one. A typical example is this sentence in which a broader ternary series of clauses contains a second ternary series within the third and last section: 'A l'intérieur, les ferrures partout reluisaient; des tapisseries dans les chambres protégeaient du froid; et les armoires regorgeaient de linge, les tonnes de vin s'empilaient dans les celliers, les coffres de chêne craquaient sous le poids des sacs d'argent' (p.80). Simpler ternary forms are everywhere: 'Tous mangeaient du pain de froment, buvaient dans des auges de pierre, et portaient un nom sonore' (p.85), 'Il tua des ours à coups de couteau, des taureaux avec la hache, des sangliers avec l'épieu' (p.86), 'Maudit! maudit! maudit!' (p.89), 'Elle grossit. Il devint fameux. On le recherchait' (p.92), 'Julien s'étala dessus complètement, bouche contre bouche, poitrine sur poitrine' (p.107). One can pick out at least sixty cases of such ternary series, the effect of which is to produce an extremely regular rhythm, in which expectations are always fulfilled and each element fits into the place assigned to it in advance. This is almost diametrically opposite to the anti-climactic disappointments which characterise so much of the rhythm of *Un Cœur simple*, but it is obviously appropriate to a hagiographical legend in which the saint's life moves ineluctably towards its appointed conclusion, in which prophecies are fulfilled, and in which nothing depends on chance.

In all these devices, Flaubert is evidently trying to conform, with the means of his own literary techniques, to the spirit of medieval art as he understood it, most notably in stained glass. Only in imposing a psychologically coherent pattern on Julien's behaviour is he leaving that behind, though there is one section where he seems to have been inspired by pastiche rather than by genuine medieval artefacts or modern adaptations of them. That is in the passage recounting Julien's adventures on leaving his parents' castle. Here the tone changes, the language becomes free and luxuriant, and the fantastic predominates. The reason is that at this point Flaubert's mind has evidently been full of reminiscences of Hugo's *Légende du Beau Pécopin* (claiming in 1856 that he was not afraid of the resemblance is in fact tantamount to admitting the potential existence of such a resemblance). In both texts we find the same piling up of sonorous names, of rolling rhythms, of improbable assertions, of mock-heroic feats, of rare terms, in which fancy combines all manner of races and countries.

But if, under Hugo's influence, Flaubert really lets himself go here, the passage also illustrates another noteworthy feature of *Saint Julien*, the tendency to include long lists and enumerations with an air of exhaustiveness. One thinks of the diverse species of hounds comprising Julien's hunting-pack, of the different birds he trains, the catalogue of animals slaughtered in the first hunt or of those which torment Julien in the second. This tendency to apparent completeness is announced near the beginning when we are told that the father's armoury contains 'des armes de tous les temps et de toutes les nations' (p.80), and the sense of order it suggests is underlined by the significant repetition of the expression 'par rang de taille' (pp.85 and 94) in reference to the father's falcons and to the animals which file past Julien in his dreams. Svend Johansen (*39*) has also noted that there are places in *Saint Julien* where Flaubert seems intent on exhausting the possibilities of different grammatical formulations in parallel phrases: 'courbés, poudreux, en habits de toile, et chacun s'appuyant sur un bâton' (p.95), 'au milieu de leur peau blanche, sur les draps du lit, par terre, le long d'un christ d'ivoire' (p.100). These devices too have their analogy in a stained-glass window, where the individual fragments are assembled so as to fill all the space available with no interstices.

There is also much more attention drawn to the images in *Saint Julien* than in *Un Cœur simple*: not only do they have a symbolic function not apparent in the first tale; they are also more than twice as frequent: 0.95 per page as compared to 0.38, and they are much more sumptuous in character. Dialogue too works quite differently. The proportion of direct speech is as small in *Saint Julien* as in *Un Cœur simple*, but far from being mechanical and cliché-ridden, it is full of significance and solemnity; as Mme Debray-Genette has written, 'tout se passe comme si on ne pouvait parler qu'un langage inspiré' (*45*, p.43). The predictions of the Hermit and the Gipsy, the stag's prophecy, the Leper's summons and ritual demands show that direct speech is reserved for the most critical moments and has an air of supernatural gravity and dignity. In these respects too, *Saint Julien* has something of the stylised but colourful formality of a stained-glass window.

The fact that catalogues, images and direct speech have a notably sonorous quality points to another characteristic feature of *Saint Julien*, its closeness to a certain type of oral narration. This aspect was given full value when Flaubert read it aloud, as Zola recalls: 'Dans les passages de force, lorsqu'il arrivait à un effet final, il montait jusqu'à un éclat de tonnerre, les plafonds tremblaient. Je lui ai entendu achever ainsi la *Légende de Saint Julien l'Hospitalier*, dans un véritable coup de foudre du plus grand effet' (*56*, p.217). Signs of orality are apparent in the text: the use of 'or' (p.92) marking the narrator's intention of introducing a new circumstance, the repetition for intensification: 'Et cela dura longtemps, très longtemps!' (p.106), 'et celui dont les bras le serraient toujours grandissait, grandissait' (p.108). Certain conventional epithets hint at a close community of traditions or systems of belief shared by narrator and reader: 'le bon seigneur' (p.80), 'notre père Adam' (p.94), 'Notre-Seigneur Jésus' (p.108). A special case is the use Flaubert makes of what he thought of, rightly or wrongly, as the ' "Et" biblique' – the 'et' standing at the beginning of a sentence. Though it is found elsewhere in *Trois Contes*, it is given special prominence in *Saint Julien* by virtue of the fact that, on the eleven occasions when it occurs, it is placed at the beginning of a paragraph, with particular frequency in the increasingly solemn closing pages. In all this, there is a tacit assumption, again as in a stained-glass window, that we are dealing with a medieval artist addressing himself to a medieval public. When the narrator appeals to common knowledge, it is invariably either to something of timeless and universal validity ('avec la facilité que l'on éprouve dans les rêves' (p.88), 'à l'heure où la brume rend les choses indistinctes' (p.91)) or to specifically medieval ideas ('huit dogues alains, bêtes formidables qui sautent au ventre des cavaliers et n'ont pas peur des lions' (p.85), 'de quelle manière on les lance, où se trouvent ordinairement leurs refuges, quels sont les vents les plus propices' (p.84)). At no point does the narrator of the main story address himself directly to the modern reader, as he does in *Un Cœur simple* when he points out that, in Félicité's time, Trouville had not developed as a resort, or suggests that, if we go there to check, we shall see that the farmyard at Geffosses really is on a slope or that the terrace in the convent looks out over the Seine.

But if the voice of the narrator of the legend itself remains firmly within the medieval convention, there is of course a second narrator, who appears at the very end and steps right outside that convention when he says: 'Et voilà l'histoire de saint Julien l'Hospitalier, telle à peu près qu'on la trouve, sur un vitrail d'église, dans mon pays' (p.108). This sentence is unique in Flaubert's fiction in that it is the only place where he uses the first person singular and admits openly that he, Gustave Flaubert, is telling a story. One reason for doing this is, as we have seen, to draw attention specifically to the relationship between this retelling of the legend and a stained-glass window. But the sentence has other functions too, emphasised by the blank which cuts it off from the foregoing narration. We are thus left in no doubt that Flaubert himself is not to be identified with the narrator responsible for the main recounting of Julien's life, who accepts with such docility all the assumptions about God, Christ and sainthood which underlie it: whence no doubt the jokes in his letters about the 'edifying' nature of the tale and the impression it will give that he is becoming a pillar of the Church. This conscious dissociation establishes a visible distance between author and work; the effect is that of a disclaimer, a refusal to accept responsibility for anything that has been said or implied in the legend.

This ostentatious distancing of himself from the story he has just related raises the difficult question of why the legend of St Julian should have appealed to Flaubert in the first place. All we have seen so far relates to the way in which Flaubert, by analogy with a stained-glass window, decided to handle the medieval legend once he had the idea of producing his own version of it. But it seems clear that he did not hit on this particular saint's life by chance. To have thought of writing it in 1846 or thereabouts, to have planned it and taken notes for it in 1856, and finally to have returned to it and composed it in 1876 indicates a strong and permanent attachment to the legend, when, apart from the very different case of St Anthony, he never seems to have shown any interest in other saints' lives. This makes it highly unlikely that he saw it merely as an aesthetic exercise, for which virtually any other hagiographical legend would have served the same purpose. Curiously, the care he takes to ensure that the reader does not attribute the legend directly to him suggests that it may have had a peculiarly personal meaning for him which he was at pains to conceal and which indeed may not have been entirely clear to him. Certainly his correspondence contains no comment about the inner sense of *Saint Julien* as it does for both *Un Cœur simple* and *Hérodias*.

Perhaps the first thing to be noticed is that the distance which Flaubert puts between himself and the legend is not overtly or necessarily ironic. He may have taken a malicious pleasure in producing, at a time of reactionary Catholic fervour, a saint's life the motive force of which is murder and bloodshed and in which the final scene has distinct sexual overtones. But if he perhaps derived sardonic amusement from the (unrealised) project of a luxury edition of the tale for the Christmas market, there is nothing in the way he tells the story to invite the reader to take a mocking attitude towards it – and it would have been very easy to induce such a response, as can be seen from the writings of Mérimée or Anatole France, for instance. Indeed, it is arguably the only thing Flaubert ever wrote in which there is no discernable irony at all, unless one counts what may rank as a mildly sarcastic dig at the pretentious self-confidence of doctors, when Julien's fear of killing his parents causes him to fall ill: 'Il manda les maîtres mires les plus fameux, lesquels ordonnèrent des quantités de drogues. Le mal de Julien, disaient-ils, avait pour cause un vent funeste, ou un désir d'amour' (p.90). Apart from that one possible case, Flaubert's normally corrosive humour is nowhere in evidence in this tale.[5]

On the other hand, it would doubtless be going too far to detect in the story any very marked nostalgia for belief. Henri Guillemin has contended that Félicité and Julien are 'des êtres brûlés de passion et de foi, des âmes tout en élan vers l'infini, des cœurs purs et qui voyaient Dieu', and that Flaubert created them with a sense of 'emportement secret, de douleur, d'impossible espoir' (8, p.148). Admittedly, in the nineteenth century, it was common enough to express regret for past ages when religious faith was unquestioned and a life-sustaining force: one finds it in writers as diverse as Lamartine, Musset, Villiers de l'Isle-Adam, Mallarmé and Huysmans, and it is not unthinkable that some shades of it can be detected in Flaubert's attitude to Félicité.[6] But Julien appears quite different and shows few signs of active faith. As a child, he remains kneeling in chapel throughout long services, but that sounds like a purely conventional attitude. Later, after his parricide, he does not revolt against God who made him commit it, but neither does he pray for divine forgiveness. Even when he decides to become a ferryman, it is part of a process of self-abasement and of inflicting suffering on himself, rather than an act undertaken in the hope of meriting divine pardon: at this point, the text tells us that

[5] Not all modern critics agree about the absence of irony from Saint Julien. P.-M. de Biasi (49, p.96), for instance, argues that there is a ludic and parodic element in the story and detects in it 'une tonalité paradoxale, plus proche du sourire et du clin d'œil que de la dérision'.

[6] Sartre sees something of the sort in Flaubert's relationship with Félicité: 'si nous interrogeons l'écrivain adulte sur sa toute première jeunesse (...), nous verrons que ce n'est pas le bonheur perdu qu'il regrette mais plutôt ce que (...) Gustave nomme "simplicité" (...). "Un cœur simple", "un cœur pur" ne se contrarie pas lui-même, il n'est pas déchiré par le conflit de la Raison et de la Foi; son mouvement naturel le porte vers le haut; il s'élève en adorant. Qui? Dieu, un Seigneur, un père, une Patronne: peu importe; c'est l'élévation qui compte, quel qu'en soit l'objet. Et cette élévation est une donnée immédiate de l'affectivité (...). Pour lui (...) la pire bêtise, c'est l'intelligence. La "servante au grand cœur" a mis son génie dans sa vie' (61, p.332).

'l'idée lui vint d'employer son existence au service des autres' (p.104) and there is no mention of God. Indeed, there is no hint that God is in his thoughts at all until the Leper reveals himself as Christ.

A somewhat less extreme view, that sees the penitent and agonised Julien as an obscure double of Flaubert himself, has no doubt more to be said for it. In Flaubert's letters, the artist is often presented as a saint or as a martyr, achieving salvation through self-sacrifice and suffering. It is thus only a step to considering Julien as an analogue of the author. This point of view has been propounded by René Jasinski, among others: 'Certes, nous n'entendons pas que Julien *soit* Flaubert. Mais que de fois affleure l'allusion! L'humble cellule du saint devant le "grand fleuve" aux "flots verdâtres" s'évoquait dans l'étroit pavillon de Croisset, devant la large courbe de la Seine. "Le besoin de se mêler à l'existence des autres le faisait descendre dans la ville"; de même, Flaubert, farouchement isolé, gagnait parfois Rouen, où bientôt l'offensaient lui aussi "l'air bestial des figures, le tapage des métiers, l'indifférence des propos". Sur lui, comme sur Julien, pesaient de douloureuses fatalités, dont la tradition romantique illustrait la grandeur; et dans ses efforts, ses dégoûts, n'attendait-il pas de l'art, foi suprême, les miraculeuses transfigurations?' (*34*, p.172). The problem with this reading is that it applies only to the latter part of the legend and leaves out of account everything up to and including the murder of the parents: that being so, while it shows Flaubert drawing on personal experiences and feelings in imagining himself in Julien's position, it provides no clue as to why the legend as a whole should apparently have meant so much to him.

Another approach, which avoids this difficulty, is to take Flaubert's interest in St Julian as involuntary, provoked by an unconscious recognition, in the legend, of his own fantasms. Such psychoanalytical interpretations take some support from the undeniable prefiguration of the second, sinister hunt in a dream which Flaubert had in 1845 and which, exceptionally, he took the trouble to record. Here it is, as he related it in his *Notes de voyage*: 'Les singes sont nos aïeux. J'ai rêvé, il y a environ trois semaines, que j'étais dans une grande forêt toute remplie de singes; ma mère se promenait avec moi. Plus nous avancions, plus il en venait; il y en avait dans les branches, qui riaient et sautaient; il en venait beaucoup dans notre chemin, et de plus en plus grands, de plus en plus nombreux. Ils me regardaient tous, j'ai fini par avoir peur. Ils nous entouraient comme dans un cercle; un a voulu me caresser et m'a pris la main, je lui ai tiré un coup de fusil à l'épaule et je l'ai fait saigner, il a poussé des hurlements affreux. Ma mère m'a dit alors: "Pourquoi le blesses-tu, ton ami? qu'est-ce qu'il t'a fait? ne vois-tu pas qu'il t'aime? comme il te ressemble!" Et le singe me regardait. Cela m'a déchiré l'âme et je me suis réveillé... me sentant de la même nature que les animaux et fraternisant avec eux d'une communion toute panthéistique et tendre' (*1*, X, p.361). The resemblances are unmistakable: the scene in a forest, the multitude of animals with their eyes fixed on the protagonist, who feels more and more threatened; the guilt at shedding the blood of animals; the ape taking Flaubert's hand as the wolf nuzzles Julien's; the association of parents with the guilt feelings; the realisation that crimes against animals are closely related to crimes against humans. With such evidence to hand, it is no wonder that a number of critics, with Sartre prominent among them, have seen *Saint Julien* as being essentially a transposition of Flaubert's obsessions and fantasms.

Sartre's argument is that *Saint Julien* is really about the killing of the father, a view supported by the detail of the fox noted above. Sartre argues that, with Julien, 's'il lui est parfaitement intolérable d'avoir tué son père par hasard, c'est qu'il sait, au fond de lui-même, qu'il n'est pas innocent, ce crime-là (...) n'a-t-il pas craint toute sa vie de vouloir le commettre?' (*61*, p.1903). If this is so, it is because Flaubert obscurely felt guilty for his own father's death: 'Julien n'accède à la sainteté que pour avoir poignardé son géniteur: c'est cette superbe méprise qui attise sa haine de soi et le pousse à l'extrême dénuement: de même Gustave ne recevra le génie que de la mort prématurée d'Achille-Cléophas' (*61*, p.1910). Summing up his case, Sartre writes: 'l'histoire de Julien, en tant qu'il a décidé de l'assumer en la racontant à neuf, s'est obscurément chargée de lui représenter la sienne, en tant que ce calice doit se boire jusqu'à la lie' (*61*, p.2128). Though Sartre's readings of Flaubert are occasionally vitiated by his cavalier attitude to biographical minutiae, what is known of Flaubert's relationship with his father, who wanted him to be a lawyer and had little respect for a career in literature, would tend to lend credibility to this interpretation of *Saint Julien*.

Other critics have developed these or similar psychoanalytical readings of *Saint Julien*, and whatever one's views of the general validity of psychoanalysis as a tool of literary criticism, in this case they have an undeniable degree of plausibility. They offer a possible explanation of Flaubert's longstanding preoccupation with the legend, they treat the legend as an indissoluble whole as it evidently appeared to him, and they help us to understand why the agonisingly personal nature of Flaubert's involvement with Julien should have induced him to hide behind not just one narrator, but two.

So *La Légende de Saint Julien l'Hospitalier* conceals turbulent depths beneath its surface impassivity: depths of which Flaubert was doubtless largely unaware and which he would certainly not have wanted his readers to discover. Hence the total refusal to drop hints or leave clues as to what may lie behind its apparent calmness and detachment and its impeccable mastery of form. To that extent, it is perhaps the most enigmatic of Flaubert's works, the one most resistant to making explicit an ulterior meaning in it. To quote Svend Johansen (*39*, p.38), 'Le mutisme de Saint Julien reste intact. Dans sa parfaite clarté, c'est une œuvre très hermétique'.

4. Hérodias

If it is possible to trace the origins of *Saint Julien* back to 1846 and maybe even further, and those of *Un Cœur simple* at least to 1849 or 1850, *Hérodias* seems to be of more recent growth. There are no positive signs of Flaubert taking an interest in the beheading of John the Baptist at any very early stage in his career, though there is evidence of a preoccupation, many years before, with an analogous biblical subject, in which eroticism mingles with decapitation. This is to be found in the comment he made in Italy in 1845 on seeing Titian's painting of Judith and Holophernes; after comparing this picture with other representations of the same scene, he goes on: 'Belle histoire que celle de Judith, et que, dans des temps plus audacieux, moi aussi, j'avais rêvée!' (*1*, X, p.367). But it is not until much later that there is any sign of the transfer of such themes to the story of Salome and John the Baptist.[7] This comes when, in a notebook primarily devoted to notes for *La Tentation de Saint Antoine* apparently taken in 1871, he unexpectedly includes several pages of notes on reading around the circumstances of John's execution. Possibly it was his re-reading of Renan's works of biblical history which gave Flaubert the idea of converting this episode into a tale, as P.-M. de Biasi has suggested (*65*, pp.537 and 646). It is possible that the recurrence of the idea in 1876 is connected with the paintings of Gustave Moreau, whom Flaubert admired and who several times treated the theme of Salome or the analogous one of the head of Orpheus: Flaubert visited the 1876 *Salon*

[7] Though there is a strange indirect link, when in 1850 Flaubert records the night he spent in Esneh with the Egyptian courtesan Kuchiuk-Hanem. The dance she had previously performed for him is clearly still in his mind when he describes Salomé's dance. It is thus not without interest to note that at the time he was already associating this experience with the story of Judith: after the dance he slept with Kuchiuk-Hanem, and his description of the night they spent together includes these sentences: 'Une autre fois, je me suis assoupi le doigt passé dans son collier, comme pour la retenir si elle s'éveillait. J'ai pensé à Judith et à Holopherne couchés ensemble' (*1*, X, p.490).

in which Moreau exhibited one of his most striking works, *L'Apparition*, showing a very dramatic Salome, at about the time his letters first mention the idea of writing the story.

At all events, by the time he had written a few pages of *Un Cœur simple*, Flaubert had decided to go on to what was to become *Hérodias*, though he hesitated over the title, either on the one hand *La Décollation de Saint Jean-Baptiste* or on the other *Hérodias* or *Hérodiade*, before finally opting for the one which did not immediately situate the story in the Christian and biblical perspective. In late April 1876, he wrote: 'Savez-vous ce que j'ai envie d'écrire après cela? L'histoire de Saint Jean-Baptiste. La vacherie d'Hérode pour Hérodias m'excite. Ce n'est encore qu'à l'état de rêve, mais j'ai bien envie de creuser cette idée-là' (*1*, XV, p.448). So from this early stage, it is clear that what interests Flaubert is the weakness of Hérode exploited by his wife (it is worth pointing out that, in Flaubert's vocabulary, 'vacherie' does not mean 'dirty trick' as it does in modern French, but is a near-synonym of 'veulerie' or 'lâcheté'). The next mention of the idea in his letters confirms this impression, and makes it clear that whatever aura of piety may have clung to *Saint Julien*, there will be none in the new tale: 'je trouve que, si je continue, j'aurai ma place parmi les lumières de l'Eglise. Je serai une des colonnes du temple. Après saint Antoine, saint Julien, et ensuite saint Jean-Baptiste, je ne sors pas des saints. Pour celui-là, je m'arrangerai de façon à ne pas "édifier". L'histoire d'Hérodias, telle que je la comprends, n'a aucun rapport avec la religion. Ce qui me séduit là-dedans, c'est la mine officielle d'Hérode (qui était un vrai préfet) et la figure farouche d'Hérodias, une sorte de Cléopâtre et de Maintenon. La question des races dominait tout' (19 June 1876; *1*, XV, p.458) .

This declaration gives us important clues as to what Flaubert saw in the story and deserves to be looked at more closely. The statement that the subject as he conceives it has no connection with religion cannot be taken literally: it would hardly be possible to recount the story of John the Baptist in such a way that it had nothing to do with religion, whether positively or negatively. What Flaubert evidently means is that he is not concerned with religion as a motivating force: non-religious factors such as race seem to him to loom much larger. And when he says that Hérode is 'un vrai préfet', this has a particular significance for him, which is clarified when one remembers that at that very time he was toying with the idea of writing a novel entitled *Monsieur le Préfet* which he had discussed with his disciple Guy de Maupassant who tells us that Flaubert 'affirmait que personne n'avait jamais compris quel personnage comique, important et inutile est un préfet' (*65*, p.87). Indeed some of the notes he took for *Hérodias* are in the same notebook as notes for *Monsieur le Préfet*, which begin as follows: 'le livre doit inspirer la Haine de l'autorité et mettre en relief l'élément officiel. Officiel: le magistrat (négation de la justice qui doit être le contraire de l'officiel)' (*1*, VIII, p.448). So Hérode is a despicable official figure, unconcerned with justice, comic and useless in his combination of important functions and weak incompetence, but important by virtue of what depends on him. As for Hérodias, she has something of Mme de Maintenon, the wife of Louis XIV who dominated his declining years, and something of Cleopatra – an allusion which takes on a special resonance when one knows that, planning in 1863 a *féerie* entitled *Le Rêve et la vie*, Flaubert had envisaged Cleopatra as one of the incarnations of what he called 'la Femme-Perdition' or 'la femme qui perd les hommes' (*62*, pp.34 and 42). In this connection, it is worth noting that also juxtaposed to notes for *Hérodias* are notes for another novel to be called *Sous Napoléon III*, which contain the significant words: 'La dégradation de l'Homme par la Femme' (*1*, VIII, p.440). These allusions strongly suggest that at the time he was elaborating his plans for *Hérodias*, Flaubert's mind was working constantly on thematic material dealing bitterly and ironically with the humiliating and ruinous domination of man by woman, in a political context. It is not surprising that transfers and contaminations should have taken place and that some of the themes relating to the Second Empire should have found their way into the biblical subject.

But whatever potentialities Flaubert may have seen in the subject, of necessity it posed problems and demanded handling in a way totally different from the other two tales. *Un Coeur simple* was an invented story set in a real milieu; *Saint Julien* was a pre-existing story set in an unrealistic milieu. The new tale was to be a historical subject set in a real place at a real time. As a consequence, however he intended to interpret the story, Flaubert had to satisfy himself that he had an intimate knowledge of historical, social, racial and religious information about Palestine at the time of Christ, and this he proceeded to acquire with his usual fanatical thoroughness. This was all the more necessary as there was no question of the selectiveness of detail one finds in *Un Cœur simple* or of filtering the information through another medium like the stained-glass window in *Saint Julien* . On the contrary, the people and places here came to him in close-up with almost hallucinatory vividness: '*Hérodias* se présente et *je vois* (nettement, comme *je vois* la Seine), la surface de la Mer Morte scintiller au soleil. Hérode et sa femme sont sur un balcon d'où l'on découvre les tuiles dorées du Temple' (17 August 1876; *1*, XV, p.485). With such distinctness of vision, it was doubly important that the detail should be right if the illusion was not to be compromised, so over a period of nearly two months, Flaubert embarked on a vast programme of reading in French, Latin and English, at least thirty volumes and articles, many of them highly technical, on topics as diverse as geography, biblical history, Roman history, archaeology, religious practices, epigraphy and numismatics, and by authors ranging from the writers of antiquity to the most modern authorities. In addition, he consulted experts, when books did not provide the information he wanted: he interviewed a leading orientalist called Clermont-Ganneau and asked him to provide disyllabic names of places visible from the fortress of Machaerus, while Flaubert's friends Baudry and Laporte were pressed into service to supply the ancient names of stars (2, pp.209-12).

However, the conscientiousness of the erudition and the outward resemblance with Renan's techniques of reconstruction in his *Histoire des origines du christianisme* should not mislead us into supposing that Flaubert had any intention of trying to reconstitute the real circumstances of the execution of John the Baptist. Hérodias is a work of fiction, and Flaubert has no scruples about altering history where it fails to provide him with the effects he desires. In practice, if one examines the situation as Flaubert outlines it in his tale, one soon notices deviations, some of them major, from known historical fact.

Contrary to what the tale tells us, Vitellius was not present at the beheading of John and was not even Governor of Syria at the time, Philip was not arming secretly, the Pharisees had not obtained the priesthood, and Machaerus may have been in the hands of the Arabs. Flaubert has not so much invented new elements as rearranged existing facts for his own purposes. Time is foreshortened so as to bring together events widely separated by chronology. But if anachronisms abound in the story, they do not result from ignorance or carelessness: Flaubert had documented himself much too thoroughly for that. Here as elsewhere, he would have denied that factual accuracy was his prime consideration. As he wrote to George Sand not long before starting work on *Hérodias*: 'je regarde comme très secondaire le détail technique, le renseignement local, enfin, le côté historique et exact des choses. Je recherche par-dessus tout la *beauté*, dont mes contemporains sont médiocrement en quête' (December 1875; *1*, XV, p.431). If there was no reason to get such details wrong, Flaubert would go to great lengths to get them right, but if they did not fit in with his aesthetic intentions, he would not hesitate to change them or, preferably, to rearrange them. The technique is the same as he had used in *Salammbô* and which Claudine Gothot-Mersch has defined in these terms: 'plutôt que celle d'*invention*, c'est donc la notion de *déplacement des données* qui permet de décrire avec quelque justesse le type de travail auquel se livre Flaubert' (*67*, p.79).

If one analyses the alterations he made to history, one sees that they follow a consistent pattern. Motivations in the biblical story are simple; in Flaubert's tale they are immensely complex, and this is because he has tampered with history with the visible intention of making Hérode's situation even more complicated and difficult by increasing the number of contradictory pressures bearing down on him. Here is the 'vrai préfet', inadequately occupying a crucial administrative position and faced with an official decision as urgent as it is vital. Iaokanann has been his prisoner for some time, and he cannot indefinitely postpone making up his mind what to do about him, whether to free him or have him executed. Hérodias hates him and longs to see him dead; Mannaeï, the Samaritan executioner, loathes him because he is a Jew; the Essenian Phanuel urges his release; the occupying Roman authorities, on whom Antipas depends, are suspicious of anything that smacks of sedition; the Pharisees, Sadducees and other sects are all agitating for their various interests; Antipas himself knows he cannot procrastinate indefinitely, but he is paralysed by the terrifying complexities of the factors he must assess in deciding what to do. It is important to remember that the reader sees all this largely as Antipas sees it; though the focus in *Hérodias* changes more than in either of the other two tales, it is Antipas whom we meet first and whose fortunes form the connecting thread of the narration. This means that we are made to share his bewilderment at all the difficulties confronting him.

Undeniably, this does not make for easy reading. The problem is twofold. On the one hand, as Flaubert well knew, his readers would have little previous familiarity with all the confused ramifications of the social, political, personal and religious situation in first-century Palestine. As he complained: 'Le difficile, là-dedans, c'est de se passer, autant que possible, d'explications indispensables' (25 October 1876; *1*, XV, p.502). Indeed, the contradictory desires to increase the complexity of the situation and to abridge the explanations as much as possible have made his text difficult to follow, and in one place even as intelligent a reader as Taine misunderstood what Flaubert was saying (*4*, p.215, n.12). On the other hand, the reader remains unsure how to handle the profusion of information laid before him. He thinks it may well prove important to assimilate it all, to remember who all the characters are, what they stand for, and how they relate to one another and to the central dilemma facing Antipas. What one must bear in mind is that this perplexity is also that of Antipas: he too despairs of making sense of all that is going on, of reconciling so many disparate sects, actions, pressure groups and personal interests. A writer other than Flaubert might have evoked the chaotic welter of elements in the situation by more impressionistic means, which could have simplified the reader's task. But that was not Flaubert's way, and the early part of the story is a jumbled mass of nuggets of information, each one of which looks as though it might be vital and all of which are presented more or less on the same level.

But if one looks at the shape of the story as a whole, it becomes

evident that all these pieces of social, political, racial and other detail
are eventually going to be swept away as irrelevant when Salomé
performs her dance. Then, all those present, forgetful of their
differences, their rivalries, their enmities, are united in stark sexual
lust for her, as is made clear in the long sentence which precedes her
request for Iaokanann's head: 'sans fléchir ses genoux, en écartant les
jambes, elle se courba si bien que son menton frôlait le plancher, et les
nomades habitués à l'abstinence, les soldats de Rome experts en
débauches, les avares publicains, les vieux prêtres aigris par les
disputes, tous, dilatant leurs narines, palpitaient de convoitise'
(p.139). One can well understand why Flaubert should have said that
he intended to make the tale 'luxurieux' (*1*, XV, p.477), and that a
crude note in the drafts should have emphasised the state of arousal in
which Antipas finds himself: 'Faire croire au lecteur qu'il va
décharger' (*1*, IV, p.596); one may indeed regret that considerations of
decency make him reticent in the finished text and induce him to
substitute rather formal literary metaphors for the physical notations
he would doubtless have preferred. But it is noteworthy that in his
version, unlike the biblical text, Antipas is not alone in being brought
to such a pitch of excitement: all the spectators are equally exalted by
Salomé's dance, though Antipas's lust has extra reasons because of
Salomé's resemblance to his wife in her lost youth, so that time and old
age are for him abolished, as a remarkable ellipsis makes clear:
'C'était Hérodias, comme autrefois dans sa jeunesse' (p.138). But
apart from that, for all of them, desire is of the same basic, physical
nature. It is no coincidence that the whole incident takes place during
a banquet, with a large part of the first section devoted to all the things
being eaten. Moreover, it is striking that in this banquet scene Flaubert
spends almost as much time talking about Aulus as he does about
Antipas – and Aulus is characterised above all by his extraordinary
gluttony, described in nauseating detail. The prominence accorded to
Aulus, whose part in the action is minimal, is clearly meant to cast his
shadow over all the proceedings, as is brought out by this startlingly
cinematographic view: 'De temps à autre, il s'étalait sur le triclinium.
Alors, ses pieds nus dominaient l'assemblée' (p.132). In this way,
Aulus, the very incarnation of fleshly appetite, implicitly

contaminates the sexual appetite of the other guests: the lust for Salomé which affects all of them is implicitly presented as an appetite of the same base, animal nature as Aulus's disgusting obsession with devouring food.

It is thus animal desire which brings about the execution of Iaokanann. The administrative decision, the complexity of which has been plaguing Antipas from the beginning, is thus wrung from him for an entirely irrelevant reason, wholly unconnected with the merits of the case, with his responsibilities as Tetrarch, or with the consequences of his action. No doubt in this he strikes Flaubert as a 'vrai préfet', a man set in authority but swayed by purely personal motives, neglectful of justice and of his proper duties. To make matters worse, he has fallen victim to a plot organised by his wife. In the whole of the banquet scene, she makes only two brief appearances: to propose a toast to Caesar and introduce her daughter, and to curse Mannaeï when at first he is too scared to kill Iaokanann. Otherwise she remains hidden in an upper gallery, the placing of which is significant. There are three levels in the banqueting hall: the floor level, occupied by the bulk of the guests; a platform for the official party of Antipas, Vitellius and Aulus; and above that the curtained gallery containing Hérodias, who has stage-managed everything. That she should thus, unseen, occupy the dominating position is obviously a deliberate piece of engineering by the author, related to the fact that, as prime mover, she gives her name to the story, even though she is by no means the focus of attention or the most prominent character.

But if Hérodias succeeds in her aim of encompassing Iaokanann's death, there is nevertheless a profound and visible irony in what she achieves. She believes that her machinations will silence Iaokanann for ever, but we as readers know that the ultimate result is exactly the opposite, Iaokanann's message will resound through the centuries, Christianity will spread irresistibly as one of the world's great religions, and Hérodias will only be remembered as the butt of the prophet's scorn and the agent of his death. So her apparent triumph is in fact her downfall and the triumph of her adversary. This compounds the irony of the whole story. One of the crucial decisions of world history is taken for ignoble and irrelevant reasons, but the person whose plotting brought about that decision has in the end set in motion a chain of events diametrically opposite to what she intended. In this context, it is important to see that Flaubert, like Renan, is considering the rise of Christianity exclusively as a historical phenomenon, in which questions of approval or disapproval do not arise. Whereas in *Saint Julien* he at least suspends his disbelief so as to present Julien as a saint, he handles John the Baptist quite differently. In the first place, our prior knowledge and expectations of him are to some extent nullified by his being referred to by the exotic and unfamiliar name of Iaokanann. Secondly, we only ever see him from the outside and are never allowed to follow his thoughts, so that we cannot know whether he is a divinely inspired prophet, a seditious agitator, a sexually obsessed reformer or a religious maniac. The text does not tell us, we have no means of knowing, and for Flaubert's purposes it does not matter. The vital and undisputed fact about him is that he played a key role in the origins and spread of Christianity.

At one stage, Flaubert had intended to underline the message of his story more explicitly than he does in the final text. As it stands, the closing sequence, after the beheading and the end of the banquet, is carefully neutral in tone. The two messengers whom Iaokanann had sent to Jesus return, and Phanuel, now converted, leaves with them: they bear away Iaokanann's head: 'Comme elle était très lourde, ils la portaient alternativement' (p.142). Certainly this first departure from the claustrophobic confines of Machaerus and the hint of an indefinite future opening up carry overtones of the coming spread of Christianity, the more so as in myth, especially that of Orpheus, a severed head may live on and prophesy. But at the same time, a purely physical explanation is available. Ever since Mannaeï returned to the hall with the head of Iaokanann, the reader's attention has been fixed on the head as an object (an aspect emphasised by the presence of gruesome physiological detail wholly absent from the vague and conventional evocation of the corpses in Saint Julien). So the last page may be read as a statement of purely material fact: the men have a long way go in the heat of the desert, the head is heavy, so they take turns in carrying it.

But while Flaubert had always intended to conclude his story with this scene, plans and drafts reveal that, over a period of time, he had been going to handle it quite differently, in a way which would have inflected the story much more towards a symbolic interpretation. Here is the most elaborate of these earlier versions: 'Ils emportent la tête sur la montagne derrière Machaerous. Soleil levant. La tête confondue avec le soleil dont elle masque le disque, des rayons ont l'air d'en partir' (*1*, IV, p.598). The effect would have been cinematographic, like that of Aulus's feet. Had Flaubert maintained this idea, the end of *Hérodias* would have been a kind of transfigurational apotheosis, strongly reminiscent of the end of *La Tentation de Saint Antoine*, published only a couple of years before: 'Le jour enfin paraît; et comme les rideaux d'un tabernacle qu'on relève, des nuages d'or en s'enroulant en larges volutes découvrent le ciel. Tout au milieu, et dans le disque même du soleil, rayonne la face de Jésus-Christ. Antoine fait le signe de la croix et se remet en prières' (*1*, IV, p.171). But in the event he decided to suppress this tableau, with its overtly mythic suggestions. All that remains, apart from the head, is the mention 'A l'instant où se levait le soleil' (p.141), and the rays have completely disappeared, though it may well have been at the moment of this change that Flaubert decided to bring them into the latter part of the banquet scene, where the description of the hall as the head is passed round contains, in an apparently climactic position, what seems a curiously pointless detail: 'Les paupières closes étaient blêmes comme des coquilles: et des candélabres à l'entour envoyaient des rayons' (p.141). This reorganisation, characteristically for the late Flaubert, throws the weight of responsibility for interpretation on to the reader. Unambiguous clues as to how to read the story are omitted, and it is up to us to decide whether we wish to see in what is recounted anything more than a physical statement about the weight of an object.

In fact, compared with *Saint Julien*, the possibility of attaching symbolic significance to given details and things (other than the head) is much reduced. With most of the other objects, it would seem arbitrary to try to subject them to a hermeneutic reading, though Margaret Tillett has sought to show that Antipas's concealed herd of white horses is related to Flaubert's conception of genius (*51*). Otherwise, though objects proliferate in *Hérodias*, their purpose is evidently to contribute to the visual clarity of what is evoked and to create the impression of an alien and exotic world. Thus the reader is confronted with numerous strange things: 'péplos' (p.137), 'cnémides' (p.122), 'gnomon' (p.133), 'chlamyde' (p.133), 'amphores' (p.135), 'atrium' (p.113), 'triclinium' (p.132), 'vélarium' (p.113), 'gerboises' (p.126), 'kiccars' (p.126), 'algumim' (p.131) and a host of other unfamiliar items. Even that which might be familiar can be transformed by an unaccustomed designation, as when, instead of calling the embossment on the Roman shields a 'bosse', he uses instead the Latin term 'umbo' (p.121). The strangeness of objects is paralleled by the strangeness of names of people. The most obvious case is of course that of 'Iaokanann', but there is also Flaubert's preference for 'Antipas' or 'le Tétrarque' rather than the 'Hérode' one would expect and which he uses in his letters. These changes serve to keep the tale at a certain distance from the biblical context and to increase the sense of a milieu in which nothing is as one expects it to be. Other names too are made to appear bizarre by a liberal use of accents, cedillas and diaereses in surprising places: 'Iaçim', 'Naâmann', 'Mannaeï', and so on. Moreover, proper names are used in great profusion – names of people, of countries, of mountains, of rivers, of stars, of cities, of races, of sects, of tribes and of gods: over a hundred and fifty in all, most of them doubtless unknown to the non-specialist. Most readers are likely to despair of retaining the significance of each of them, even if they have access to an annotated edition, which was not Flaubert's intention. But for Antipas this too is a world full of confusion and uncertainties, dominated by the unknown and the alien, in which he feels lonely and threatened. The confusion of languages heightens this impression. Some of the characters speak Latin, others Syriac, others again Greek, with the consequent necessity of interpreters to translate for them. There is even a whole line of verse in Latin. This cacophony of languages and races is brought out by the unusually high proportion of the story which consists of direct speech: about one fifth of the whole, compared to an insignificant proportion in the other two tales, and twice as much as one finds in *Salammbô*, the work most directly comparable to *Hérodias*. The novels set in modern times show a similar proportion but not distributed in the same way:

it has been calculated by Gothot-Mersch (*64*) that in these novels the average length of pieces of direct speech varies from 1.7 lines in *L'Education sentimentale* to 2.3 in *Madame Bovary*, whereas here it is something like 6.5. *Hérodias* is thus, of all Flaubert's works, the one in which the characters are most eloquent. This derives in large part from the zest with which Flaubert has created the vehement pseudo-biblical rhetoric of Iaokanann. He remarked with satisfaction of this tale: 'Ça se présente sous les apparences d'un fort gueuloir, car, en somme, il n'y a que ça: la Gueulade, l'Emphase, l'Hyperbole. Soyons échevelés!' (14 December 1876; *1*, XV, p.510), or a few days later: 'C'est peu "naturaliste", mais "ça se gueule", qualité supérieure' (*1*, XV, p.515), and what struck Edmond de Goncourt when Flaubert read it aloud was 'les beuglements du liseur' (*60*, II, p.1171). Not that this higher degree of direct speech implies more real communication between the characters: quite the opposite. Phanuel's prediction is couched in such ambivalent terms that Antipas misunderstands it; Antipas and Hérodias only trade insults and wounding allusions; the banquet is a perpetual crossfire of angry remarks, denunciations, exclamations and exhortations. The effect of the whole is one of noisy discord; as Debray-Genette notes: '*Hérodias*, au contraire des autres contes, semble rempli du bruit et de la fureur des paroles directement rapportées' (*11*, p.44).

Too many conflicting interests and emotions are drawn together in the stifling atmosphere of Machaerus for there ever to be a real meeting of minds or exchange of views. A similar sense of juxtaposition without organic connection is produced by the frequency of evocations of pointlessly swirling motion: 'Les portières des corridors furent agitées comme par le vent. Une rumeur emplit le château, un vacarme de gens qui couraient, de meubles qu'on traînait, d'argenteries s'écroulant, et, du haut des tours, des buccins sonnaient, pour avertir les esclaves dispersés' (p.118); 'Les plus voisins de la porte descendirent sur le sentier, d'autres le montaient: ils refluèrent, deux courants se croisaient dans cette masse d'hommes qui oscillait, comprimée par l'enceinte des murs' (p.121). A similar device leads Flaubert to create paragraphs consisting of juxtaposed but contrasting elements, with no clear links between them: 'Antipas se renversa comme frappé en pleine poitrine. Les Sadducéens avaient bondi sur Jacob. Eléazar pérorait, pour se faire écouter' (p.134); 'Vitellius la compara à Mnester, le pantomime. Aulus vomissait encore. Le Tétrarque se perdait dans un rêve, et ne songeait plus à Hérodias. Il crut la voir près des Sadducéens. La vision s'éloigna' (p.138). Even the changing point of view in the story increases the feeling of disparateness, of a universe which lacks a unifying factor of sense. Though Antipas is undoubtedly at the centre, the focus changes unpredictably, so that at different times we see things from the viewpoints of Hérodias, of Vitellius, of Aulus, of Phanuel, of various minor characters. Such diversity is most unusual in a short story, and contrasts strongly with the other two, where the focus remains unremittingly on Félicité and Julien. Once again, the reader is confronted with the difficulty of mastering and comprehending so much densely packed material. As Debray-Genette has put it: 'l'obscurité est le principe même de l'écriture (...) Le conte est obscur parce qu'il doit traiter de l'obscurité' (*52*, p.339).

In addition to the shape previously analysed, the intensifying complexity of the pressures affecting Antipas and their sudden effacement by the lust everyone feels for Salomé, *Hérodias* contains some other features which help to bind together so many disparate elements. One is the three appearances of Phanuel. At the end of the first part, Phanuel, who is an Essenian (that is, in Flaubert's view, a member of a pre-Christian sect) comes to Antipas to plead for Iaokanann's release and to tell him something vital – but is interrupted before he can say what it is. Then, towards the end of the second part, he returns to announce that the stars presage the death of an important man that very night in Machaerus. Finally, he is the last person to be mentioned as the guests file out of the banqueting-hall, leaving Antipas, his head in his hands, staring fixedly at the severed head of Iaokanann, 'tandis que Phanuel, debout au milieu de la grande nef, murmurait des prières, les bras étendus' (p.141). His attitude, that of the crucified Christ and the use of the nerm 'nef', usually reserved for ecclesiastical architecture, bring out the religious overtones of his presence and lead into the last page where Phanuel, converted, joins the two messengers to bear the head off to Galilee.

A similar thread is supplied by the mentions of Salomé. In her first exchange with Antipas, Hérodias alludes briefly and mysteriously to her daughter whom she has abandoned for Antipas's sake. Salomé then appears anonymously when Antipas sees, on the flat roof of a house near his citadel, a girl whose face is hidden but whose lithe body excites his desire: 'Il épiait le retour de ce mouvement, et sa respiration devenait plus forte, des flammes s'allumaient dans ses yeux' (p.116). At the end of the second part, she makes an equally fleeting and nameless appearance in Hérodias's apartments, when a girl's arm comes through a curtain, gracefully trying to reach a tunic. When an old woman picks it up, Antipas is struck by the feeling that he has seen her before and asks Hérodias if it is her slave, to receive an evasive answer. But even a perspicacious reader may not at this stage realise that it is the same old woman who had been holding a parasol to shade the girl on the roof. It is only after Salomé's dance that we are given the key to the enigma. Salomé takes the severed head up to the gallery in which Hérodias is concealed, and a few minutes later the head reappears 'rapportée par cette vieille femme que le Tétrarque avait distinguée le matin sur la plate-forme d'une maison, et tantôt dans la chambre d'Hérodias' (p.141). But this revelation is one for Antipas too: knowing now that the old woman belongs to Hérodias and has been attending Salomé, it becomes belatedly clear to him that he has been the victim of a plot laid by his wife, which makes all the more shattering the shame he feels for having ordered the execution of Iaokanann. Not only has he committed a heinous crime for no valid reason, he has been tricked into it by a woman he hates and who despises him.

It is indeed the 'dégradation de l'Homme par la Femme', a degradation foreshadowed by the devaluing of virtually all the characters by comparisons with animals. Images in general are much more frequent and more striking in *Hérodias* than in the other two tales: 0.39 per page in *Un Cœur simple*, 0.95 in *Saint Julien* and 1.47 in *Hérodias*: according to Don Demorest, 'les images sont plus fréquentes dans ce conte que *dans toute* autre œuvre imprimée de Flaubert' (*6*, p.589). But apart from the greater brilliance of style which this gives, it should be noted that a substantial proportion of them compare people to animals: Mannaeï has 'la souplesse d'un singe' (p.111); Iaokanann displays 'l'air tranquille d'une bête malade' (p.112), and compares himself to 'un ours, un âne sauvage' (p.127); his denunciations of Hérodias liken her to 'une cavale' (p.127) and 'une chienne' (p.128); the slaves at the banquet are 'alertes comme des chiens' (p.131); the guests' arms stretch out for food 'comme des cous de vautour' (p.132); Sisenna, chief of the publicans, has '[une] mâchoire de fouine' (p.124); the Pharisees look like 'bouledogues' (p.136); Salomé in her dance is compared to a 'papillon' (p.138) and a 'grand scarabée' (p.139). All this, with the leitmotiv of Aulus sleeping, stuffing himself, vomiting, and stuffing himself again, tends to reduce the participants to the level of animals, the more so as animals are a significant part of the setting. Antipas sees horses in the Arab camp; eagles fly overhead; Iaokanann is wrapped in the skin of a camel; mules carry the Pharisees and Sadducees up to Machaerus; Antipas's treasures include both white horses and dromedaries; doves fly around the courtyard; among the food at the banquet are antelopes, storks, blue fish, bull's kidneys, dormice, nightingales, blackbirds, wild asses and lamb's tails; and Hérodias appears at the banquet between two sculpted lions and later 'les deux lions sculptés semblaient mordre ses épaules et rugir comme elle' (p.140).

Something of this theme may be taken up in a startling symbolic tableau which seems to hint that Aulus embodies a secret key to the understanding of all that happens. This occurs when the severed head is being passed round the banqueting-hall. It is first taken, off-stage, to Hérodias. Then it is set before Antipas who averts his eyes, and Vitellius who gives it a cursory glance. The Roman captains examine it with the practised precision of specialists in killing. A Pharisee handles it with detached curiosity, after which Mannaeï places it before Aulus, 'qui en fut réveillé' (p.141) (we do not know when he fell asleep: the last we heard of him was during the dance, 'Aulus vomissait encore' (p.138), so he may have missed the climax of Salomé's performance). Flaubert then comments: 'Par l'ouverture de leurs cils, les prunelles mortes et les prunelles éteintes semblaient se dire quelque chose' (p.141). This seems to be a distant indication that the unspoken comment which passes between the dead eyes and the eyes dulled by debauchery may carry the silent message of the whole tale. But with exemplary restraint, Flaubert withholds the slightest clue as to what it could be. The reader is free to imagine all sorts of possibilities: the reduction of the prophet and the glutton to the same inanimate level, or it may mark the coming triumph of Christian spirituality (since Aulus is destined to become Emperor); it may be the recognition of the futility of all human effort. All interpretations are possible, none is authorised by the text.

If the duplication of the narrator in *Saint Julien* increases the opacity of that text, the opacity of *Hérodias* is increased by the self-effacing reticence of the narrator. He tacitly admits that he knows Palestine (as Flaubert did) by the use of the present tense in the description of the panorama seen from Machaerus, when we are told that the desert 'figure, dans le bouleversement de ses terrains, des amphithéâtres et des palais abattus' (p.112). He supplies, rather intrusively, one piece of information extraneous to the actual narration when he tells us that Iaokanann is 'le même que les Latins appellent Saint Jean-Baptiste' (p.111), which implies standing outside the temporal framework of the story, since the appellation 'Saint' did not apply in John's lifetime. Likewise, he looks forward to the subsequent history of Aulus whose gluttony 'devait surprendre l'univers' (p.121). Other present tenses betoken a momentary identification with the beliefs of the time evoked, when he refers to 'le baaras qui rend invulnérable' (p.133), to 'ce promontoire de la Scandinavie où les dieux apparaissent avec les rayons de leurs figures' (p.135), and perhaps to 'des queues de brebis syriennes, qui sont des paquets de graisse' (p.137). But there are no aphorisms or generalisations to orientate our ideas, no expressions of opinion about the characters, no first or second person pronouns designed to bring narrator and reader closer together.

The same opacity is apparent in Flaubert's decision to elide what might have been the logical climax of the story, namely the scene when Iaokanann's head is at last set before Hérodias, marking the success of her plot and her apparent triumph. We see Salomé carry the head up to the gallery in which her mother is hidden, and we see the old slave bring it back and hand it to Mannaeï, but we see nothing of the reactions of Hérodias, though it is she who gives her name to the story. Equally, Salomé is dismissed once she has fulfilled her function of seducing Antipas into ordering the execution of a man whose name she cannot even remember. One can divine some of the advantages which accrue from this ellipsis. Had Flaubert transported us into Hérodias's lair, which, though in the hall, is isolated from its main body, he would have weakened the intense spatial concentration of the last part which otherwise confines the action within the walls of the hall, until the opening out when the head is borne away into the distance of space and time. It would also have directed our attention to Hérodias's presumable reactions of cruel joy and satisfaction, when he has otherwise ensured that we regard her only as an agent, a catalyst for action, and do not take too much interest in her motives or feelings for their own sake. So he would have weakened the dramatic intensity of *Hérodias*, which very much recalls classical tragedy in the prominence accorded to dialogue, in the obvious division into scenes, in the observance of the unities of time and space. But by this ellipsis, Flaubert also heightens the sense of impenetrable mystery which hangs over the tale; what could have been *the* decisive event of the story is elided, which has led Gérard Genette to the perhaps extreme conclusion that '*Hérodias* is *unreadable*' (55, p.201). But the ellipsis also enables Flaubert to displace the climax of the tale. If one compares *Hérodias* to Oscar Wilde's *Salomé* or the Richard Strauss opera based on it, one sees that Wilde has sought to go beyond the horror of the beheading of Iaokanann and surpass it with an even more horrific climax in Salomé's erotic hymning of the head and Hérode's appalled command: 'Tuez cette femme!', upon which the soldiers crush her beneath their shields. Instead, Flaubert prefers a sudden and unexpected decrescendo: the lights go out, the guests depart, and we are left with the desolate picture of the three men carrying the head across the desert. Perhaps the elimination of the symbolic or mythic effect of the sun's rays is part of this scheme for a very muted ending: it both avoids repeating the effect of the conclusion of *Saint Antoine* and varies the way in which the third tale ends, when the first two had both culminated in transformations, with the parrot transformed into the Holy Ghost and the Leper into Christ. Whatever the reasons, the elision of the scene with Hérodias produces a curious syncopation in the rhythm of the tale, where so much in its plethora of motivations remains hidden from our eyes and can only be supplied by imagination and reflexion.

Because of its extraordinarily dense texture and because of its necessary obscurity, *Hérodias* has never been as popular as *Un Cœur simple* or *Saint Julien*. On publication of *Trois Contes*, the critics were almost unanimous in declaring *Un Cœur simple* and *Saint Julien* to be masterpieces, while many of them condemned *Hérodias* as incomprehensible. Francisque Sarcey, widely regarded at the time as 'le prince de la critique', thought as badly of *Hérodias* as he had of *Saint Antoine*, and according to a report of a lecture he gave, 'Il n'a pas plus compris l'un que l'autre de ces ouvrages; il n'en distingue pas le but, il n'en reconnaît pas l'utilité; il se demande pourquoi ils ont été écrits' (2, p.243). For the critic of *Le XIXe Siècle*, 'Il y a là trop d'archéologie pour que le lecteur se sente fortement ému, l'œuvre est étrange plutôt que vivante et humaine' (2, p.242). In the opinion of Jules Lemaitre, 'un effort excessif se fait sentir dans cette brièveté; les personnages et les actions ne sont pas assez expliqués; il y a trop de laconisme dans ce papillotage asiatique' (2, p.247). Others dismissed it even more summarily: the critic of *L'Union* preferred not to speak of it at all, and in *La Revue suisse*, the comment was simply: 'Quant à *Hérodias*... hélas!' (3, p.189). Such severity soon went out of fashion, but it is nevertheless noticeable that modern criticism has tended to shy away from *Hérodias*; three or four times as many learned articles have been devoted to the other two as have to *Hérodias*, and many readers still regard it as unduly compact and difficult.

The reasons for this relative disfavour are not hard to discern. *Hérodias* does not have the warm humanity of *Un Cœur simple* or the glowing colours of *Saint Julien*, its appeal is less obvious and less immediate, and Flaubert has not gone out of his way to facilitate the reader's task. But once one has gone beyond the surface problems, once one realises that, despite the title and despite the fame of John the Baptist and Salomé, it is really about the weak and pathetic figure of Antipas, one begins to see that *Hérodias*, in all its bitter irony, its disillusioned view of humanity, its multifarious implications and its taut drama, is no less rich a work than its two companion-pieces. Indeed, it is arguably the most typically Flaubertian of the three: *Saint Julien* is not comparable with anything else he wrote, and *Un Cœur simple* was consciously composed as an exception to his usual manner, whereas the harsh and often misanthropic bleakness of *Hérodias* is not different in kind from that which informs the major novels. It is as if, after the catastrophes of 1875, he had been obliged to recuperate by treating less overtly depressing subjects, but with the return of confidence in his own creative powers, he had once again found the strength to revert to the uncompromising vision of the world he had always had.

5. Unity or Diversity?

Ever since the volume *Trois Contes* appeared in 1877, critics have been asking whether it is a unified work or whether the three tales are separate and unrelated. Given Flaubert's known preoccupation with the architecture of his books, the general tendency has been to suppose that in some way the three texts belong together organically and constitute a coherent whole, though opinions have varied enormously as to what the link might be. But before we consider this vexed question, it is vital to posit some preliminary facts.

The first is that the three tales, so far as is known, were first conceived at widely separated intervals in Flaubert's life: *Saint Julien* in 1846 or earlier, *Un Cœur simple* at some indeterminate time well before 1875, and *Hérodias* probably in 1871. It is also clear that Flaubert did not originally plan to write three tales which would belong together: he saw *Saint Julien* as a work on its own, he then decided to add *Un Cœur simple*, and only subsequently did it occur to him to compose a third story to go with the other two. Not only that: in 1878 and 1879 he was extremely keen on the idea of a separate luxury edition of *Saint Julien*, and only the publisher's changes of mind prevented the realisation of this project. This means that Flaubert saw no objection to isolating one of the tales from the other two and having it read as an independent entity. But while these facts rule out any notion that Flaubert envisaged the work as a triptych from the start, and while they undoubtedly prove that any theory of unity must be subordinate to the autonomous existence of its three elements, they do not preclude the possibility that he visualised *Un Cœur simple* as completing *Saint Julien* and *Hérodias* as complementary to the other two.

With these premises in mind, let us see what theories of unity have been propounded. First in the field was Flaubert's friend

Théodore de Banville, who on 14 May 1877 wrote in *Le National*: 'Les *Trois Contes* (...) ne sont pas cependant des contes détachés: ils sont unis au contraire par un lien étroit, qui est l'exaltation de la charité, de la bonté inconsciente et surnaturelle' (2, p.235). But while this case may be arguable for the first two, it founders on *Hérodias*, from which charity and supernatural kindness are conspicuously absent. But what may be variants on this view, with very different implications, can be found in some modern critics. Jasinski, for instance, puts forward the argument that all three are 'contes hagiographiques, puisqu'ils évoquent dans leurs péripéties les plus signifiantes la vie de trois saints'(*10*, p.119). For *Saint Julien* this is self-evident, and for *Un Cœur simple* it is clearly plausible to see Félicité as a kind of lay saint, and if sainthood as such is not much in evidence in *Hérodias*, Iaokanann is undeniably 'le même que les Latins appellent Saint Jean-Baptiste'. But Jasinski goes on to maintain that these apparently hagiographic tales serve a subversive purpose. He claims that with Félicité, 'le principe de sa sainteté est une bêtise congénitale' (p.120), and that with Julien 'sa sainteté (...) tient à un principe non moins probant: la cruauté' (p.121), while 'la sainteté de saint Jean-Baptiste s'authentifie par la virulence de ses haines' (p.121). These considerations lead Jasinski to conclude that 'l'intention militante ne fait pas de doute. Le pieux triptyque entend édifier sur les récits édifiants' (*10*, p.123). There is certainly some merit in these arguments, but while they rightly recognise the cynical implications of *Hérodias*, they lay too much stress on the negative elements in *Un Cœur simple* and *Saint Julien*. Despite Flaubert's notorious hatred of 'bêtise', what he detested most was the 'bêtise' of intellectuals, whereas he had some sympathy with the more animal-like 'bêtise' which is Félicité's. As for Julien, it is by no means clear that in the nexus of guilt and expiation on which the legend depends his cruelty is wholly condemnable.

Another variant on Banville's exaltation of charity is put forward by Per Nykrog, who maintains that: 'Les *Trois Contes* reproduisent, en ordre inverse, les caractéristiques théologiques des trois personnes de la Sainte Trinité, incarnées dans des figures humaines'. According to his reading, for Flaubert, 'le christianisme, compris d'une façon non-dogmatique et séparé de l'Eglise, occupe

une place de tout premier ordre dans l'histoire mentale de l'humanité'
(*12*, pp.60 and 66). Here the difficulty is rather that Iaokanann is not
the centre of the story in which he is involved. A view closer to that of
Jasinski is that proposed by J. van de Ghinste, who finds the
differences between the tales as illuminating as the common ground.
'Dans chaque cas, tous les éléments qui, dans Saint Julien, contribuent
à réaliser la perfection de la légende sont, dans les deux autres contes,
réduits à la réalité la plus prosaïque. Dans *Hérodias*, la grandeur et la
simplicité sont sournoisement sapées par les équivoques et les
turpitudes. Dans *Un Cœur simple*, le monde chrétien contemporain,
tout en subissant une idéalisation naïve dans l'imagination de Félicité,
est présenté comme mesquin et illusoire' (*16*, p.8). In fact such are the
discrepancies between these different attempts to relate the *Trois
Contes* to one another on the basis of their handling of the theme of
religion, especially Christianity, that they are unlikely to command
sufficient assent to establish that the volume has a real thematic unity.

Perhaps in recognition of this difficulty, some recent
commentators have sought to establish thematic links between the
three stories without postulating any one of them as dominant. Thus
one finds Michael Issacharoff writing: 'Il est clair que les éléments
symboliques des *Trois Contes* – parole, regard, feu, espace –
rattachent chaque récit aux deux autres' (*14*, p.39), and in somewhat
similar vein, the editor of the newest edition of *Trois Contes* maintains
that: 'Les *Trois Contes*, loin de constituer trois œuvres séparées,
possèdent une réelle unité thématique' (*5*, p.81), and proceeds to
examine the thematic links, in a good quarter of his introduction, under
some eight separate headings. That certain thematic similarities can be
detected is undeniable, but it is doubtful whether they are any more
significant than those which might be found between any three works
of Flaubert chosen at random.

Another approach to the problem of unity is to see the three
stories, whatever their divergences, adding up to form a panoramic
work. On the simplest level, that of chronology, this view finds support
from the 1856 letter in which Flaubert talks to Bouilhet about *Saint
Julien*, and, thinking of the imminent publication of *Madame Bovary*
and his proposed revision of *La Tentation de Saint Antoine*, he goes on:

'si j'étais un gars, je m'en retournerais à Paris au mois d'octobre avec le *Saint Antoine* fini et le *Saint Julien* écrit. Je pourrais donc en 1857 fournir du moderne, du moyen âge et de l'antiquité' (*1*, XIII, p.522). This of course is exactly what he does, twenty years later, and in the same order: modern times, Middle Ages and antiquity. So there may well be a sense in which the three tales complete one another to present a panoramic view of humanity through the ages. Related to this view is Albert Thibaudet's contention that the three tales represent three ways of making history into art: daily reality, where everyday detail looms so large that no historical perspective emerges, legend, where the distance is so great that myth and fiction take over from verifiable fact, and real history, where facts are clearly assembled into a meaningful pattern (*7*, p.196). But this interpretation tends to break down when one realises that *Hérodias* is anything but faithfully observed historical reality, whatever impression it may convey.

Two other related explanations for the co-existence of the *Trois Contes* in the same book may be mentioned, though neither postulates any real unity. One is that the aging Flaubert's inspiration was flagging and that he could no longer do anything but repeat on a smaller scale his old achievements. Thus it is suggested that *Un Cœur simple* is an echo of *Madame Bovary*, that *Saint Julien* repeats *Saint Antoine*, and that *Hérodias* is a miniaturised copy of *Salammbô*. Admittedly, there is a kind of symbiosis of *Madame Bovary* and *Un Cœur simple*, and Flaubert was uncomfortably aware that *Hérodias* risked repeating some of the effects of *Salammbô*: 'Tous mes efforts tendent à ne pas faire ressembler ce conte-là à *Salammbô*' (31 December 1876; *1*, XV, p.520). However, apart from the fact that both works take a saint as their main character, *Saint Julien* and *La Tentation* have little in common: they deal with totally different ages and civilisations, and the thematic material is utterly dissimilar. A comparable view is that set forth by Maxime Du Camp, who claims that all three subjects are old and associated with Flaubert's native province: 'Il y avait longtemps que ces trois histoires hantaient sa cervelle. *Saint Julien l'Hospitalier* a été conçu à la vue d'un vitrail d'église normande: *Hérodias* a été inspiré par les sculptures d'un des portails latéraux de la cathédrale de Rouen, et le *Cœur simple* est le développement d'un récit qu'il avait entendu à Honfleur' (*57*, II, pp.390-91). That *Saint Julien* relates to the Rouen window is announced by Flaubert himself, and there is too a connection between *Hérodias* and the bas-relief representing Salome's dance above the north door of the cathedral; it shows Salome in exactly the attitude depicted by Flaubert and is mentioned as 'Marianne dansant' (its popular designation in Rouen) when the guide is showing Léon and Emma round the cathedral in *Madame Bovary* (*1*, I, p.262), but we have only Du Camp's word for it that *Un Cœur simple* originates in an anecdote heard at Honfleur, and it is well known that he was intent on demonstrating that Flaubert's epileptic attack in 1844 had dried up his inspiration and that everything he wrote had been conceived before then. So, while his evidence cannot be dismissed, it must be treated with great caution.

In any case, even if the tales depend on old subjects and do contain echoes of earlier writings, the fact remains that each of them is an experimental work and represents a new departure. Never before had Flaubert attempted anything comparable to his adaptation of a medieval legend in *Saint Julien*, the deliberate reconciliation of his pessimism and a consolatory effect in *Un Cœur simple*, or the reduction of a whole crowded world to a few dense pages in *Hérodias*. The fact is that *Trois Contes* without doubt add something new to the Flaubert canon and that our image of him as a writer would be radically different if he had never written them.

As far as unity is concerned, though a number of the hypotheses advanced to establish a case for it are ingenious and at least partly persuasive, nearly all of them do violence to one or more of the tales in trying to weld them into a coherent whole. Given that any considerations of unity must, as we have seen, remain subordinate to recognition of the essential autonomy of each of the three stories, it seems prudent not to attach too much importance to such a controversial issue. Indeed, it may be precisely because they are different that Flaubert believed that they could be put together in a single volume. In 1842, he had written to his schoolmaster and mentor Gourgaud-Dugazon: 'j'ai dans la tête trois romans, trois contes de genres tout différents et demandant une manière toute particulière d'être écrits' (*1*, XII, p.386), which, perhaps coincidentally, sounds strangely like a programme for the 1877 volume. The three tales are clearly differentiated by style as much as by theme (in Flaubert the two are always inseparable), and the differentiation produces deliberate contrasts. It is thus perhaps not entirely fanciful to think of the three stories as being complementary precisely because of their differences, in something of the same way in which the movements of a symphony complete one another, by their differences in theme, in key, in tempo and in orchestration.

Ultimately, though, questions of this sort are of secondary importance, and what matters most is that the tales, taken individually, are all masterpieces, Whether or not one accepts his view of the connection between them, there is no reason to dissent from the opinion expressed over a century ago by Théodore de Banville: 'ces contes sont trois chefs-d'œuvre absolus et parfaits, créés avec la puissance d'un poète sûr de son art' (2, p.234).

Select Bibliography

The secondary literature devoted to Flaubert and *Trois Contes* is so abundant that there could be no question of presenting anything like a complete list here; what follows is thus highly selective. Of the numerous general studies on Flaubert containing chapters on *Trois Contes* (such as those by Digeon, Brombert, Bart, Starkie, Tillett and Nadeau), I have included only those specifically quoted in this volume. As for books and articles on *Trois Contes,* I have for reasons of space, restricted myself to mentioning those which I have found particularly useful or from which I have quoted, but the absence of a given item from this list should not be taken to mean an adverse judgement on its value. A more extensive bibliography may be found in 5 below. Within each section, items are listed in chronological order; place of publication of books is only given when it is somewhere other than Paris.

EDITIONS OF COMPLETE WORKS
1. *Œuvres complètes*, Club de l'Honnête Homme, 16 vols, 1971-76.

EDITIONS OF 'TROIS CONTES'
2. Conard (ed. L. Biernawski), 1921.
3. Bordas (ed. R. Decesse), 1959.
4. Harrap (ed. C. Duckworth), London, 1959, frequently reprinted.
5. Classiques Garnier (ed. P.M. Wetherill), 1988.

GENERAL STUDIES OF FLAUBERT QUOTED HERE
6. Demorest, D., *L'Expression figurée et symbolique dans l'œuvre de Flaubert* (Presses modernes, 1931; Geneva, Slatkine Reprints, 1967).
7. Thibaudet, A. *Gustave Flaubert* (Gallimard, 1935).
8. Guillemin, H., *Flaubert devant la vie et devant Dieu* (Plon, 1939; new ed. Nizet, 1963).

STUDIES OF 'TROIS CONTES'

9. Cigada, S., 'I *Trois Contes* nella storia dell'arte flaubertiana', *Contributi del seminario di filologia moderna (seria francese)*, 1961, pp.252-69.

10. Jasinski, R., 'Le Sens des *Trois Contes*' in *Essays in Honor of L.F. Solano*, Chapel Hill, University of North Carolina Press, 1970, pp.117-28

11. Debray-Genette, R., 'Du mode narratif dans les *Trois Contes*', *Littérature*, 2 (mai 1971), pp.39-62.

12. Nykrog, P., 'Les *Trois Contes* dans l'évolution de la structure thématique chez Flaubert', *Romantisme*, 6 (1973), pp.55-66.

13. Raitt, A.W., 'Flaubert and the art of the short story', in *Essays by Divers Hands,* London, Oxford University Press, 1975, pp.112-26.

14. Issacharoff, M., '*Trois Contes* et le problème de la non-linéarité', *Littérature*, 15 (1975), pp.27-41.

15. Carlut, C., P.H. Dubé and J.R. Dugan, *Concordance to Flaubert's 'Trois Contes'*, New York , Garland, 1980.

16. Ghinste, J. van de, 'L'Unité des *Trois Contes*', *French Studies in Southern Africa,* 10 (1981) pp.3-12.

17. Raitt, A.W., 'Les Styles de Flaubert dans *Trois Contes*' in *Mélanges de littérature française offerts à M. Shackleton et C.J. Greshoff,* University of Cape Town, 1985, pp.52-76.

STUDIES OF 'UN CŒUR SIMPLE'

18. Gérard-Gailly, *Le Grand Amour de Flaubert,* Aubier, 1944.

19. Cento, A., 'Il "plan primitivo" di *Un Cœur simple*', *Studi francesi,* 13 (gennaio-aprile 1961), pp.101-03.

20. Johansen, S., 'Ecritures d'*Un Cœur simple*', *Revue romane*, fasc.II (1967), pp.108-20.

21. Raitt, A.W., Commentary on an extract from *Un Cœur simple* in *The Art of Criticism: Essays in French Literary Analysis,* Edinburgh, Edinburgh University Press, 1969, pp.205-15.

22. Debray-Genette, R., 'Les Figures du récit dans *Un Cœur simple*', *Poétique*, 3 (1970), pp.348-64.

23. Wake, C., 'Flaubert's search for an identity: some reflections on *Un Cœur simple*', *French Review*, Vol.XLIV, Special Issue No. 2 (Winter 1971), pp.89-96.

24. Willenbrink, G., *The Dossier of Flaubert's 'Un Cœur simple'*, Amsterdam, Rodopi, 1976.

25. Fleury, F., *Plans, notes et scénarios de 'Un Cœur simple'*, Rouen, Lecerf, 1977

26. Debray-Genette, R., 'La technique romanesque de Flaubert dans *Un Cœur simple*: étude de genèse' in *Langages de Flaubert*, Minard, 1976, pp.95-108.

27.   Fairlie, A., 'La contradiction créatrice: quelques remarques sur la genèse d'*Un Cœur simple*', *Essais sur Flaubert,* Nizet, 1979, pp.203-32.

28.   Bonaccorso, G., et al., *Un Cœur simple*, Les Belles lettres, 1983.

29.   Debray-Genette, R., '*Un Cœur simple* ou comment faire une fin: étude des manuscrits', *Gustave Flaubert I: Flaubert, et après...,* Minard, 1984, pp.105-33.

30.   Barnes, J., *Flaubert's Parrot,* London, Cape, 1984.

31.   Debray-Genette, R., 'Le roman d'*Un Cœur simple*' in *Gustave Flaubert e il pensiero del suo secolo,* Messina, Università di Messina, 1985, pp.7-19.

32.   Fairlie, A., 'Facettes de la pensée de Flaubert à travers les manuscrits d'*Un Cœur simple*', ibid., pp.21-36.

STUDIES OF 'LA LÉGENDE DE SAINT JULIEN L'HOSPITALIER'

33.   Descharmes, R., '*Saint Julien l'Hospitalier* et *Pécopin*', *Revue biblio-iconographique,* III, 12 (1905), pp.1-7, 67-75.

34.   Jasinski, R., 'Sur le *Saint Julien l'Hospitalier* de Flaubert', *Revue d'Histoire de la Philosophie,* 3 (15 avril 1935), pp.156-72.

35.   Vinaver, E., 'Flaubert and the legend of St Julian', *Bulletin of the John Rylands Library Manchester,* 36 (September 1953), pp.228-44.

36.   Cigada, S., 'L'episodio del lebbroso in *Saint Julien l'Hospitalier* di Flaubert', *Aevum,* XXXI, 5-6 (settembre-dicembre 1957), pp.465-91.

37.   Raitt, A.W., 'The Composition of Flaubert's *La Légende de saint Julien l'Hospitalier*', *French Studies,* XIX, 4 (October 1965), pp.358-72.

38.   Duckworth, C., 'Flaubert and the legend of St Julian: a non-exclusive view of sources', *French Studies,* XXII, 2 (April 1968), pp.107-13.

39.   Johansen, S., 'Ecriture et fiction dans *Saint Julien l'Hospitalier*', *Revue romane,* III, 1 (1968), pp.30-51.

40.   Vinaver, E., '*La Légende de Saint Julien l'Hospitalier* et le problème du roman', *Bulletin de l'Académie de Langue et de Littérature françaises,* 3-4 (1970), pp.107-22.

41.   Bart, B.F., 'Psyche into myth: humanity and animality in Flaubert's *Saint Julien*', *Kentucky Romance Quarterly,* XX, 3 (1973), pp.317-42.

42.   Pilkington, A.E., 'Point of view in Flaubert's *La Légende de saint Julien l'Hospitalier*', *French Studies,* XXIX, 3 (July 1975), pp.266-79.

43.   Strike, W.N., 'Art et poésie dans *Saint Julien l'Hospitalier*', *French Studies in Southern Africa,* 5 (1976), pp.52-63.

44. Bart, B.F., and R.F. Cook, *The Legendary Sources of Flaubert's 'Saint Julien'*, University of Toronto Press, 1977.
45. Debray-Genette, R., *'La Légende de saint Julien l'Hospitalier:* forme simple et forme savante', *Essais sur Flaubert*, Nizet, 1979, pp.233-51.
46. Berg, E.J., G. Moskos and M. Grimaud, *Saint/Oedipus. Psychoanalytical Approaches to Flaubert's Art*, Ithaca and London, Cornell University Press, 1982.
47. Vanhese, G., 'Archaïsme et Histoire dans *La Légende de saint Julien l'Hospitalier*', *Micromégas*, IX, 3 (settembre-dicembre 1982), pp.147-71.
48. De Biasi, P.-M., 'La pratique flaubertienne du symbole' in *Gustave Flaubert e il pensiero del suo secolo*, Università di Messina, 1985, pp.248-70.
49. ——, 'Le palimpseste hagiographique. L'appropriation ludique des sources édifiantes dans la rédaction de *La Légende de saint Julien l'Hospitalier*', *Gustave Flaubert 2*, Minard, 1986, pp.69-124.

STUDIES OF 'HÉRODIAS'
50. Lowe, M., and C. Burns, 'Flaubert's *Hérodias* – a new evaluation', *Montjoie*, I, 1 (May 1953), pp.9-15.
51. Tillett, M., 'An approach to *Hérodias*', *French Studies*, XXI, 1 (January 1967) pp.24-31.
52. Debray-Genette, R., 'Re-présentation d'*Hérodias*' in *La Production du sens chez Flaubert*, Union Générale d'Editions, 1975, pp.328-44.
53. Lowe, M., '*Hérodias*, "roman du Second Empire" ', *French Studies Bulletin*, 1 (Winter 1981-82), pp.9-11.
54. ——, '*Hérodias*, the Second Empire and "la tête d'Orphée" ', *French Studies Bulletin*, 3 (Summer 1982), pp.6-7.
55. Genette, G., 'Demotivation in *Hérodias*' in *Flaubert and postmodernism*, Lincoln and London, University of Nebraska Press, 1984, pp.192-201.

OTHER WORKS QUOTED
56. Zola, E., *Les Romanciers naturalistes*, Charpentier, 1895.
57. Du Camp, M., *Souvenirs littéraires,* 3e édition, Hachette, 1906.
58. Commanville, C., *Souvenirs intimes* in G. Flaubert, *Correspondance I*, Conard, 1926.
59. Flaubert, G., *Madame Bovary, nouvelle version*, ed. J. Pommier et G. Leleu, Corti, 1949.
60. Goncourt, E. et J. de, *Journal*, ed. R. Ricatte, Fasquelle-Flammarion, 1956.

61.   Sartre, J.-P., *L'Idiot de la famille*, Gallimard, 1971-72.

62.   Flaubert, G., *Le Rêve et la vie*, ed. K.S. Kovacs, Lexington, French Forum, 1982.

63.   Flaubert, G., et G. Sand, *Correspondance*, ed. A. Jacobs, Flammarion, 1981.

64.   Gothot-Mersch, C., 'La parole des personnages dans les romans de Flaubert', *Revue d'Histoire Littéraire de la France*, 81e année, 4-5 (juillet-octobre 1981), pp.542-62.

65.   Maupassant, G. de, *Pour Gustave Flaubert*, Brussels, Editions Complexe, 1986.

66.   Flaubert, G., *Carnets de travail*, ed. P.-M. de Biasi, Balland, 1988.

67.   Gothot-Mersch, C., 'Notes sur l'invention dans *Salammbô*' in *Flaubert, l'autre*, Lyon, Presses Universitaires de Lyon, 1989, pp.75-84.

CRITICAL GUIDES TO FRENCH TEXTS

edited by

Roger Little, Wolfgang van Emden, David Williams